Crete

by Susie Boulton

Susie Boulton first got to know Crete on a
Greek island-hopping holiday over 20
years ago. Since then she has written travel
features and contributions to guide books
on the island. A graduate of Cambridge
University, where she studied languages
and history of art, she is a freelance travel
writer and author of guide books to
Venice, Lisbon, the Algarve, Malta and
other European destinations.

Above: *a proud Cretan*

KT-155-714

AA Publishing

Above: *horse-riding is an ideal way to experience the beauty of the Cretan countryside*

Find out more about AA Publishing and the wide range of travel publications and services the AA provides by visiting our website at www.theAA.com/ bookshop

Written by Susie Boulton

First published 1999. Reprinted Nov 1999
Reprinted Apr and Aug 2000; Feb 2001
Reprinted 2001. Information verified and updated
Reprinted May and Aug 2002
Reprinted 2004. Information verified and updated.
Reprinted May, Jul and Dec 2004

© Automobile Association Developments Limited 1999
Maps © Automobile Association Developments Limited 2001

Published by AA Publishing, a trading name of Automobile Association Developments Limited, whose registered office is Southwood East, Apollo Rise, Farnborough, Hampshire GU14 OJW. Registered number 1878835.

Automobile Association Developments Limited retains the copyright in the original edition © 1999 and in all subsequent editions, reprints and amendments

A CIP catalogue record for this book is available from the British Library.

A02483

Colour separation: Pace Colour, Southampton

Printed and bound in Italy by Printer Trento S.r.l.

Contents

About this Book

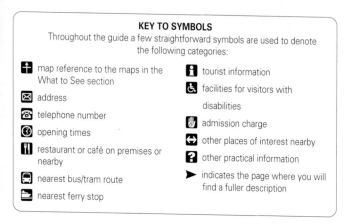

KEY TO SYMBOLS

Throughout the guide a few straightforward symbols are used to denote the following categories:

✚ map reference to the maps in the What to See section

✉ address

☎ telephone number

⏰ opening times

🍴 restaurant or café on premises or nearby

🚌 nearest bus/tram route

⛴ nearest ferry stop

ℹ tourist information

♿ facilities for visitors with disabilities

✋ admission charge

↔ other places of interest nearby

❓ other practical information

▶ indicates the page where you will find a fuller description

This book is divided into five sections to cover the most important aspects of your visit to Crete.

Viewing Crete pages 5–14
An introduction to Crete by the author
  Features of Crete
  Essence of Crete
  The Shaping of Crete
  Peace and Quiet
  Crete's Famous

Top Ten pages 15–26
The author's choice of the Top Ten places to see in Crete, each with practical information.

What to See pages 27–92
The four main areas of Crete, each with its own brief introduction and an alphabetical listing of the main attractions.
  Practical information
  Snippets of 'Did You Know...' information
  5 suggested walks
  3 suggested tours
  3 features

Where To... pages 93–116
Detailed listings of the best places to eat, stay, shop, take the children and be entertained.

Practical Matters pages 117–24
A highly visual section containing essential travel information.

Maps
All map references are to the individual maps found in the What to See section of this guide.
For example, Spinalóga has the reference ✚ 29E2 – indicating the page on which the map is located and the grid square in which the island is to be found. A list of the maps that have been used in this travel guide can be found in the index.

Prices
Where appropriate, an indication of the cost of an establishment is given by **£** signs:
£££ denotes higher prices, **££** denotes average prices, while **£** denotes lower charges.

Star Ratings
Most of the places described in this book have been given a separate rating:
✪✪✪   Do not miss
✪✪   Highly recommended
✪   Worth seeing

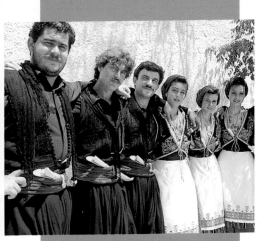

Viewing Crete

Above:
*Cretan
costumes
are still worn
on special
occasions*
Right: *the
Greek flag*

5

Susie Boulton's Crete

'Big Island'

To the rest of Greece, Crete is known as *Megalonissos* – the Big Island. It is the largest of all the Greek islands and the fifth largest in the Mediterranean. The mountain ranges which form a backbone through the centre of the island create a spectacular backdrop, particularly the Levká Óri (White Mountains) in the west, which are snow capped six months of the year.

More than any other island in the Mediterranean, Crete has the power to arouse the imagination. Ancient ruins and the exquisite works of art they have revealed offer a tantalising glimpse of Europe's first great civilisation: the highly sophisticated Minoans who built the great palace of Knosós, alleged home of King Minos and the Minotaur. The ruins of a Dorian city-state, the mighty ramparts of Venetian fortresses, the soaring minarets of Ottoman mosques, all survive as eloquent evidence of later foreign powers, lured by the island's strategic maritime setting.

Steeped in myth, history and traditions, Crete is also an island of golden beaches and blue seas which has grown to cater for an annual invasion of 2 million visitors. The sands of the north are now skirted by high-rise development, yet in the south small, remote settlements are tucked between spectacular cliffs and the Libyan Sea, some only accessible by ferry or fishing boat. Untouched too is the spectacular mountainous interior of the island where locals go by donkey, Byzantine churches glow with frescoes and rustic villages are lost in time.

Fiercely proud, with a passion for freedom and independence, the islanders regard themselves first as Cretans, secondly as Greeks. Relaxed and friendly, they will readily offer the visitor a glass of *raki*, a slice of raisin bread or a bunch of grapes. It is this warm hospitality, combined with ancient history, natural beauty and sparkling seas, that make the island, quite simply, unforgettable.

Travelling by donkey is still a way of life in the villages of rural Crete

Features of Crete

Geography
• Crete is long and thin, extending 250km from east to west and varying from 12km to 60km from north to south.
• Crete has 1,046km of coastline.
• Apart from the tiny outpost of Gávdos, Crete is the most southerly of the Greek islands.
• Crete has about 300 days of sunshine a year.

Population
• The population of Crete is 550,000.
• Roughly half the population live in the administrative district of Irákleio, a quarter in Chaniá and an eighth in both Réthymno and Lasíthiou.
• Most of the population live on the north coast.

Government
• Crete is an administrative district of Greece, and sends elected deputies to the Athens parliament.
• The island is divided into four provinces: Chaniá, Réthymno, Irákleio and Lasíthiou.
• Each province has a governor, appointed by the Greek Government in Athens.

Tourism
• Tourism is overtaking agriculture as the main source of income. Exports of fruit and vegetables are on the decline as more and more coastal villages turn to tourism.
• Of the 2 million plus tourists that visit Crete annually, the majority are German, followed by Scandinavians and British.

The towering 'iron gates' of the Samariá Gorge. Thousands of visitors make the 16km walk each year

Off-season Tourism
Crete's tourist season currently lasts only seven months, from Easter to October. The island is keen to benefit from a longer holiday season but is unable to do so without making improvements to its infrastructure. Currently, for example, there is insufficient electricity to sustain winter tourism and too few activities to offer tourists. Consequently the island is embarking on a winter pilot programme, with the emphasis on sports, health programmes, cultural and ecological pursuits.

Essence of Crete

Left: *Chieftan Cup from Agía Triáda, in the Museum of Archaeology at Irákleio*
Below: *soaking up the sun in Chaniá*

The proud and unyielding character of the Cretan has been shaped by many years of sieges, battles and famines; but the warmth and hospitality of the people are shaped, above all, by the Mediterranean climate. Long mornings are followed by a leisurely lunch and a siesta of two or three hours. Business resumes until about 8PM when it is time for the *vólta* or evening stroll. If there's one thing the locals love it's a fiesta, and they enthusiastically participate in saints' days and other religious festivals. Visitors to the island are more than welcome to join in.

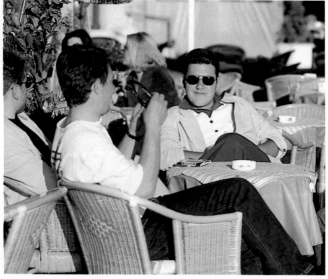

THE **10** ESSENTIALS

If you only have a short time to visit Crete, or would like to get a really complete picture of the island, here are the essentials:

• **Learn about Minoan civilisation on Crete** by soaking up the atmosphere of the palace of Knosós (➤ 22) then viewing the wonderful displays in Irákleio's Archaeological Museum (➤ 17–18).

• **Wander around Chaniá**, one of Crete's most attractive towns, then take some time to relax in a café or taverna looking out over the picturesque harbour.

• **Join in the dancing** at a typical Cretan evening in a country taverna – an impromptu event with the locals is best, but even those which have been staged for tourists offer an infectious brand of Cretan fun.

• **Hike down the spectacular Samariá Gorge** – a demanding, but almost compulsory day out (➤ 20, 83).

• **Conjure up images of marauding pirates** at the Venetian fortress in Réthymno, then explore the ancient streets.

• **Head for the hills**, and discover absolute seclusion amid magnificent scenery in one of the rugged mountain ranges – the Levká Óri (White Mountains), the Ída Mountains or the Díkti massif.

• **Take a boat trip** around the coast to see otherwise inaccessible beaches and coves, or take a ferry or caïque to an offshore island.

• **Savour a simple meal** of freshly caught fish and a glass or two of Cretan wine, while gazing out over the sea from a taverna with a view.

• **Go to market** in Irákleio or Chaniá and be tempted by the enormous range of herbs, spices, rakí and honey – the perfect place to make up a picnic.

• **Take to the streets at festival time** – there are lots of opportunities throughout the year to see colourful processions, fireworks and Cretans having a good time.

Above left: *Knosós ruins: the restored horns of consecration (left) are a symbol of the sacred bull*
Above: *the wild and rugged landscape near the great cave of Kamáres, in the Ída Mountains*

The stalls of the morning market at Odós 1866 in Irákleio cater for all tastes

9

The Shaping of Crete

6000 BC
Arrival of Crete's first inhabitants, probably from Asia Minor or the Levant. The main settlement of these neolithic cave-dwellers is Knosós.

c3000 BC
Beginnings of the great Minoan civilisation, known as the Pre-Palatial period. Ceramics, tools, weapons and jewellery produced by craftsmen.

2200 BC
Start of Middle Minoan or Proto-Palatial period. First appearance of hieroglyphics.

2000–1800 BC
Construction of the first palaces at Knosós, Faistós, Mália and Zákros.

1700 BC
A natural catastrophe destroys the first palaces of the Minoan civilisation, but new ones are subsequently built on their foundations, marking the Neo-Palatial period.

c1450 BC
Palaces and towns destroyed by an unknown disaster (➤ 42). Knosós partially destroyed, but reoccupied. Mycenaeans invade Crete. This marks the beginning of the Late Minoan or Post-Palatial period, a period of decadence when the Minoan culture was kept alive in only a few areas of the island.

1370 BC
Final destruction of Knosós, probably by Mycenaeans.

1230–1150 BC
Breakdown of settled conditions on Crete and mainland Greece.

11th century BC
Dorian invasions. End of Bronze Age and start of urban civilisations.

Late 4th century BC to 1st century AD
Hellenistic period – Cretan cities vie with each other.

65 BC
Romans complete conquest of Crete; Gortýs becomes the new capital.

AD 47
St Paul driven ashore during his journey to Rome; Crete is soon converted to Christianity.

395
Division of the Roman Empire; Crete passes to the Eastern Empire under Byzantium.

824
The Arabs take Crete.

961
The Byzantine Empire reconquers Crete.

1204
Crete passes to Venice after the Venetian conquest of Byzantium during the Fourth Crusade.

Painting in the Historical Museum, Irákleio, showing the Turkish fleet off Crete

British soldiers preparing for the air defence of Crete in 1941

1210
Venetians make Candia (now Irákleio) their Cretan capital.

1453
With the fall of Constantinople to the Turks, many refugees, including artists, arrive on the island, marking the start of the Cretan Renaissance.

1645
The Turks attack Crete, capturing Chaniá and Réthymno.

1669
Candia surrenders after a 20-year siege. Final Ottoman annexation when Venetians, who have been supported by the Knights of St John of Jerusalem, evacuate the island.

1821
Cretan uprising against the Ottomans during the Greek War of Independence (1821–30).

1866
Several hundred Cretans, under siege by Turkish troops, die heroically – along with many of their aggressors – in the explosion at Moní Arkadíou.

1878
First excavations at the Palace of Knosós.

1897–8
Crete and Greece unite against the Turks who are ejected from the island. Crete becomes autonomous under a High Commissioner, Prince George, son of the King of Greece.

1900
Sir Arthur Evans begins excavations at Knosós. Work also begins at the Faistós site.

1913
Crete is annexed to mainland Greece as part of the terms of the Treaty of London.

1941
Battle of Crete. German airborne invasion of the island. Heavy losses on both sides.

1944
Germans withdraw from the island.

1945
Liberation of Crete.

1960s
Tourist boom begins. Hotels are constructed on the north coast. From 1967–74 Greece is under a military dictatorship.

1981
Greece joins the EC.

1986
Greece becomes a full member of the EC, and EC funds are used for the restoration of Cretan churches and monasteries.

2001
Greece joins the euro currency area.

Peace & Quiet

A bee enjoying the nectar of the cistus (rock rose), which grows wild in the Cretan countryside

Wild flowers on hills, mountain slopes and coastal plains create colourful scenes in spring

Peace and Quiet

Crete's varied landscape, from coastal plains to mountain plateaux and peaks, provides endless prospects for nature-lovers and walkers. Botanists flock to the island in March and April, when the slopes and coastal strips are covered with wild flowers; birdwatchers come to see migratory species in spring and rare birds of prey throughout the year. Walkers have a choice of ancient rural footpaths, spectacular gorge walks and serious hikes in the mountains. Those in search of peace and quiet should avoid the summer months, when tourism is at its height. This is also the time when the landscape is parched by the intense heat of the sun.

Flora

Thanks to its southern Mediterranean climate and variety of habitat, Crete has an extraordinary diversity of plant life. There are over 1,500 species, a significant number of which are indigenous to the island. In spring hills and mountain slopes are a carpet of wild flowers: yellow anenomes, pink and white *cistus*, blue campanulas, wild irises, orchids and clematis; on the coast there are poppies, stocks and small campions; in the fields flax, poppies, asphodels and wild tulips. In summer the land is hot and lifeless, but autumn brings flowering cyclamen, autumn crocus and sea squill. The Samariá Gorge (► 20, 83) is particularly rich in plant life, including the Cretan cyclamen, the *clusius* peony and the Cretan ebony, a shrub unique to Crete with beautiful pinkish-purple flowers. Much of the landscape consists of *phrígana*, the equivalent of the French *garigue* – a stony, open habitat of scrub and shrub, rich in wild flowers including the beautiful bee orchid and herbs such as oregano, marjoram, rosemary, sage and thyme.

Birds

Crete is a key stopping-off point for migrant species

making their way from North Africa to their breeding grounds in northern Europe. The best months to see them are March, April and May. Where there are wetlands you may see migratory waders such as avocets, sandpipers and ringed plovers, as well as year-round resident species such as marsh harriers, herons, little egrets and oyster-catchers. In the mountains eagles and vultures soar above valleys, gorges and plateaux.

Snow-capped mountains form the backdrop to the ruined hilltop city of Aptera, east of Soúda

Walking

Walking is one of the best ways of seeing the island. Easily the most popular walk is the Samariá Gorge (► 20, 83), open from May to October, but it is not for those who are seeking solitude. The Levká Óri (White Mountains) in the west of the island and the Psiloreítis range, southwest of Irákleio, offer the best mountain walks. Specialist companies offer organised half-day or day-long walks with an experienced guide (► 115), and serious climbers can contact the mountaineering clubs (► 115). If you're planning your own walk in the mountains you'll need suitable footwear, a hat, sunscreen, a whistle and extra water. You should also take a map and compass and know how to use them. The best time for walking is April and May when the weather is warm, but not too hot, and wild flowers adorn the wayside.
Autumn is good too, though the countryside is less rewarding.

Watch out for birds of prey soaring over mountains and gorges. The largest is the lammergeier

13

Crete's Famous

Zeus
Mythical Zeus, King of the Greek Gods, is Crete's ancient hero. Born in the Díktaean Cave (► 49), he led a revolt against the Titans, dethroned his father Kronos (King of the Titans), and divided the world. His brothers Hades and Poseidon were given the underworld and the seas respectively, while Zeus kept the heavens, becoming the God of the Universe.

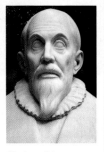

The bust of the celebrated painter El Greco (Doménico Theotokópoulos) in El Greco Park, Irákleio

El Greco

Doménico Theotokópoulos (c1541–1614), more familiarly known as El Greco, was born in Crete in about 1541. As a young artist he went to Venice and studied under Titian, then moved to Rome where he came under the influence of Michelangelo, Raphael and the Mannerists of central Italy. From 1577 El Greco lived in Spain, working mainly in Toledo. He is best known for his passionate and often disturbing Mannerist paintings. See also Fódele ► 38.

Níkos Kazantzákis

The writer and poet Níkos Kazantzákis (1883–1957) was born in Irákleio but spent most of his life abroad. Regarded as the leading Greek writer of his time, he produced novels, travel journals, poetry and philosophical essays, as well as translating western classics into modern Greek. His best known novels, both set in Crete, are *Zorba the Greek*, which became a famous film, and *Freedom or Death*. In 1957 he narrowly missed being awarded the Nobel Prize for Literature. He died in Germany a few months later and is buried on the old town walls of Irákleio (► 35). See also Myrtía ► 42.

Sir Arthur Evans

The British archaeologist Sir Arthur Evans (1851–1941) came to Crete in 1894, intrigued by the discovery on the island of ancient coins and stone seals with hieroglyphics. With an inherited fortune he bought the site of Knosós (► 22) and in 1900 began his excavations. Major discoveries were immediately made, causing a sensation throughout Europe. Evans devoted the rest of his life to Knosós, publishing his research in the six-volume work, *The Palace of Minos*. His reconstructions of the palace have incited much controversy, but his work has greatly advanced the study of European prehistory.

Sir Arthur Evans with a copy of the bull's head rhyton, now displayed in the Archaeological Museum, Irákleio

Top Ten

Above: *Thrapsanó vases have been famous for centuries*
Right: *Harvester vase from Agía Triáda in the Archaeological Museum, Irákleio*

1
Agía Triáda
(Minoan Summer Palace)

Linked to Faistós by paved road, the dramatically sited Agía Triáda is believed to have been the summer palace of Minoan royalty.

 28C1

 3km west of Faistós

 (28920) 91360

 Sep–Jun daily (except Mon) 8:30–3; Jul–Aug daily 8–7

 Café (£) at Faistós

 Buses only as far as Faistós (3km)

 None (many steps, not suitable)

Moderate

Faistós (➤ 19), Museum of Cretan Ethnology at Vóroi (➤ 43)

The ruins of Agía Triáda hint at a past splendour – a royal villa, perhaps, or a summer retreat

Close to the more famous Minoan palace of Faistós (➤ 19), Agía Triáda enjoys an equally if not more spectacular setting, on a slope overlooking the Bay of Mésaras. Far fewer tourists come here, and it is a delightful spot to explore. There is no record of the Minoan name ('Agía Triáda' is the name of a nearby Byzantine chapel) and the purpose of another palace so close to Faistós remains a mystery. The setting, which in Minoan times would have been far closer to the sea, and the elaborate decoration of the apartments, suggest this was a luxurious summer villa, possibly for use by the royalty of Faistós. The original 'palace' was razed to the ground in the disaster of 1450 BC (➤ 10, 42) and was not rebuilt until some 200 years later.

The best starting point is the Byzantine chapel. From here you can look down on the complex: to the left the grandest, sea-view apartments, which had flagstoned floors, gypsum and alabaster-faced walls, and in the corner room, fine frescoes. To the right is a group of storerooms with *pithoi* (large storage jars) and further to the right the main reception rooms. On the far side of the palace lie the ruins of a town with a porticoed row of shops.

Some of the most exquisite Minoan works of art in Irákleio's Archaeological Museum (➤ 17–18) were found here. These include three carved black stone vases (the Harvester Vase, Boxer Vase and the Chieftain Cup) and a painted sarcophagus depicting a burial procession.

2
Archaiologikó Mouseío
Ground Floor, Irákleio

The museum contains the world's richest collection of Minoan art, providing a vivid insight into the everyday life of a highly cultured society.

The rich collection of archaeological finds spans ten centuries, from early neolithic to Roman times; but the main emphasis is on the Minoan era, with treasures from Knosós, Faistós and other ancient palaces of Crete. The dreary 1960s museum building hardly does justice to this remarkable collection, and the sparse labelling and information makes the purchase of a guide essential, but the wealth of exhibits warrants more than one visit, perhaps concentrating on the ground floor galleries in the morning and the upstairs Hall of the Frescoes (see opposite) later in the day when the crowds have subsided. Tickets can be re-used on the same day. A visit to Knosós (➤ 22–3) before or after a tour of the museum (ideally both) will give a more complete picture of the Minoan civilisation.

The range of exhibits is enormous, from votive figurines, seal stones, cult vessels and gold jewellery to spearheads and sarcophagi. Outstanding are the exquisite pottery vessels of the Early and New Palace periods, and the tiny figures of animals and people, who are portrayed with an extraordinary degree of naturalistic detail. Among the individual highlights are the Faistós Disc (➤ 19) in Room III in a single case, the tiny faience figures of the bare-breasted Snake Goddesses (Case 50), the bull's head *rhyton*, or ceremonial vessel (Case 51) and the tiny ivory acrobat in mid-air (Case 56), all in Room IV; and the three carved *rhytons* from Agía Triáda (➤ 16) in Room VII: the Chieftain Cup, the Harvester Vase and the Boxer Vase.

+ 36C2

✉ Plateía Eleuthérias (entrance on Odós Xanthoudídou), Irákleio

☎ (2810) 226092

🕐 Apr–Oct Tue–Sun 8–7, Mon 12:30–7; Nov–Mar Tue–Sun 8–5, Mon 12:30–5

🍴 Cafeteria (£) beside the museum

🚌 Bus stop by the museum

ℹ Opposite the museum

♿ Ground floor only

✋ Expensive; free on Sun in winter

Top: *the Snake Goddess in a religious ritual*
Above: *the Faistós Disc, whose symbols remain undeciphered*

3
Archaiologikó Mouseío
Hall of Frescoes, Irákleio

 36C2

 Plateía Elefthérias (entrance on Odós Xanthoudídou), Irákleio

 (2810) 226092

 Apr–Oct Tue–Sun 8–7, Mon 12:30–7; Nov–Mar Tue–Sun 8–5, Mon 12:30–5

 Cafeteria (£) beside the museum

 Bus stop by the museum

 Opposite the museum

 Ground floor only

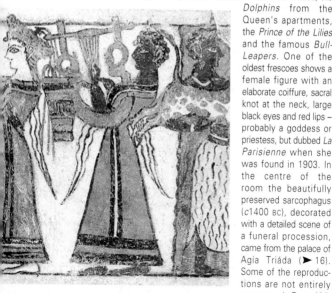 Expensive; free on Sun in winter

The greatest form of Minoan artistic achievement, the palace frescoes depict vivid scenes of nature, religious themes and the rites of court life.

The collection of magnificent Minoan frescoes, mostly from the Palace of Knosós, is the highlight of the museum; for although they are heavily restored the lively, vividly coloured works of art go to the heart of Minoan life. Dating from 1600–1400 BC the frescoes are joyful, elegant depictions of man in harmony with nature, of ceremonies and worship and scenes of daily life. Only tiny fragments of the frescoes survive, the rest is cleverly reconstructed to give a full picture. The originals were painted straight on to wet plaster, and the colour came from the dyes of plants and minerals. Following the Egyptian models, figures were painted in profile – men in red, women white and monkeys in blue.

Those who have already visited Knosós may recognise many of the frescoes from the reproductions there, including *The Cup-Bearer* from the Procession fresco, the *Dolphins* from the Queen's apartments, the *Prince of the Lilies* and the famous *Bull-Leapers*. One of the oldest frescoes shows a female figure with an elaborate coiffure, sacral knot at the neck, large black eyes and red lips – probably a goddess or priestess, but dubbed *La Parisienne* when she was found in 1903. In the centre of the room the beautifully preserved sarcophagus (*c*1400 BC), decorated with a detailed scene of a funeral procession, came from the palace of Agía Triáda (➤ 16). Some of the reproductions are not entirely accurate – in Room XVI, for example, *The Saffron Gatherer* shows a boy picking flowers – but restorers later found that the original fresco actually depicted a monkey.

Detail from the sarcophagus discovered at Agía Triáda

4
Faistós

Second only to Knosós in importance, Faistós dominated the Mesará Plain and was ruled by the legendary Rhadamanthys, brother of King Mínos.

The most striking feature of Faistós is its dramatic setting, on a ridge overlooking the rich Mesará Plain. Excavations by an Italian archaeologist in the early 20th century revealed that the development of Faistós followed that of Knosós: the original palace was built around 1900 BC, destroyed in 1700 BC and replaced by a grander palace. Unlike Knosós, however, this second palace (destroyed in 1450 BC) incorporated foundations from the first palace. This makes interpretation of the site somewhat confusing and time-consuming and there are no reconstructions (as at Knosós) to help, but the leaflet which comes with the admission ticket is quite useful.

Steps down from the entrance lead to the west court and theatre area via the upper court. The storage structures visible to the south of the west court were probably used for grain. The grand staircase leads up to the New Palace, with rooms overlooking the Old Palace (fenced off and still undergoing excavation). The huge paved central court, which has fine views of the Psiloreítis range of mountains, was originally bordered by a portico, foundations of which can still be seen. To the north the royal apartments (closed) were the most elaborate of the rooms, with the best views. It was in one of the chambers beyond these apartments, at the northern edge of the site, that the excavators discovered the famous Faistós Disc, now in Irákleio's Archaeological Museum (► 17). Small, round and made of clay, the disc is inscribed with spiralling hieroglyphics that to this day defy translation.

The north court of the Minoan palace of Faistós, in a magnificent setting looking out over the Massará Plain

➕ 28C1

✉ Faistós, Irákleio (66km southwest of Irákleio, 8km west of Moíres)

☎ (28920) 91315

🕐 Daily in summer 8–7; Oct–Apr 8–5

🍴 Cafeteria (£) on the premises

🚌 Regular service from Irákleio

ℹ Tourist Pavilion on the premises

♿ None (lots of steps)

✋ Expensive

↔ Agía Triáda (► 16), Museum of Ethnology at Vóroi (► 43)

5
Farángi Samariás
(Samariá Gorge)

28B2

43km south of Chaniá

(2810) 92287 or (2810) 67140

May—Oct, depending on weather, 6AM–sunset

Tavernas (££) at head of gorge and at Agía Rouméli; take refreshments for the gorge

From Chaniá to the head of the gorge on the Omalós Plain. From Chóra Sfakíon back to Chaniá; check times locally

In summer 4–5 ferries a day from Agía Rouméli to Chóra Sfakíon; daily afternoon ferry to Soúgia and Palaiochorá

Head of the gorge

None

Expensive

For details of walk ➤ 83

Towering peaks, plunging depths and springs of clear water – a dramatic setting for a walk through one of Europe's longest and deepest canyons.

In high season up to 2,000 tourists a day walk the 16km gorge, making it the second most popular Cretan experience after Knosós. The flood of walkers, mostly on guided tours, kills any real sense of adventure but the stunning mountain scenery is well worth the effort of the 5–7 hour hike. The gorge was designated a national park in 1962 in an attempt to preserve its wealth of flora and fauna. Most importantly the park was created to protect the famous Cretan wild goats, shy, nimble-footed animals that are unlikely to show themselves in the gorge.

The starting point at the head of the gorge is on the mountain-ringed Omalós plain, and by far the best plan is to arrive by public transport, hike through the gorge to Agía Rouméli and take a ferry from here to Chóra Sfakíon, then a bus back to Chaniá, the nearest main resort. The walk can be quite demanding, particularly in the midsummer sun, and there are mules and a helicopter on hand to help those in trouble. Sturdy shoes are essential for negotiating the scree and crossing the river. Those daunted by the prospect of a 16km hike but eager to see the gorge have two options: either to do the first part of the walk, taking the breathtaking descent down the *xilóskala* ('wooden stairs'), with the disadvantage of the stiff climb back; or to start from Agía Rouméli, climbing 2km to get to the entrance, then continuing uphill into the gorge.

6
Gortýs

The ancient ruins, scattered among fields and hillsides, are eloquent evidence of the size and power of the former capital of Crete.

Below: *the ruined basilica at Ágios Titos dominates the entrance to the city*

Not so ancient as the famous Minoan sites – in fact, rather insignificant in those days – Gortýs came to prominence under the Dorians, ousted Faistós from its pinnacle by the 3rd century BC and attained the ultimate status of capital of Crete after the Roman invasion of 6 BC. Its tentacles of power reached as far away as North Africa, but in AD 824 the great city was destroyed by the Turks, and it has lain abandoned ever since.

Though the walls have crumbled and the columns have fallen, the extensive remains are a compelling evocation of the great city. The finely preserved apse of the 6th-century Basilica of Ágios Títos is built on the supposed site of martyrdom of St Titus, who was sent by St Paul to convert the islanders to Christianity.

Nearby is the semi-circular Odeon, roofless now, but once a covered theatre where the Romans enjoyed musical concerts. And behind it, protected now by a modern brick arcade, are perhaps the most precious remains of the site – the huge stone blocks engraved with the famous law code of Gortýs which, dating from 500 BC, represents the first known code of law in Europe. In its archaic Dorian dialect, written from right to left on one line, then from left to right on the next, the code deals with civil issues such as divorce, adultery, inheritance and property rights, giving a fascinating insight into Dorian life on Crete.

The remnants of the acropolis lie on a hill to the west, and there are more remains along the road towards Agía Déka (but no parking there).

Left: *the scenic Samariá Gorge, from Omalós*

✠ 29D1

✉ Agía Déka, Irákleio (46km south of Irákleio, 8km east of Moíres)

☎ (28920) 31144

🕐 May–Oct 8–7; Nov–Apr 8–6

🍴 Café/bar (£)

🚌 Regular service from Irákleio

♿ Few

✋ Moderate; free on Sun in winter

21

7

Knosós

 29D2

 5km south of Irákleio

 (2810) 231940

Daily 8–7 (5 in winter)

Café on the site (££), tavernas nearby

No 2 from Irákleio (Bus Station A) every 10 minutes

Good (access as far as the main court)

 Expensive

Irákleio (➤ 31–7), Myrtiá (➤ 42)

Guided tours available in four languages. Shop with books and reproductions of finds from Knosós

An up-close look at Minoan remains

The Minoan civilisation grew and prospered around Knosós, the largest and most powerful of the palaces in Crete.

A hundred years ago King Minos and Knosós were merely names from the myths of ancient Greece, but in 1894 British archaeologist Arthur Evans purchased a site that transpired to be the largest and most important palace in Crete and gave credence to the myths. Excavations, which began in 1900, revealed a 13,000sq m complex of buildings, surrounded by a town of around 12,000 inhabitants. The elaborate rooms and the wealth of treasures discovered were evidence of a highly developed ancient civilisation, but it was the labyrinth layout and the sacred symbols on walls and pillars that suggested Knosós as the seat of the legendary King Minos and home of the Minotaur. Hence Evans gave the name 'Minoan' to the newly discovered culture.

Knosós and other Minoan palaces on Crete were founded around 1900 BC but destroyed in about 1700 BC, probably by a series of earthquakes. They were rebuilt but devastated again in 1450 BC, Knosós suffering least damage. The final catastrophe came in about 1375 BC and Knosós was never rebuilt.

The palace was more than the residence of royalty – it was the seat of administration and justice, an important commercial centre and a centre of religious ceremonies and rituals, with excavations revealing chapels and shrines, sacred signs and small statues representing goddesses.

Evans came under heavy criticism for his restoration of Knosós, particularly for his liberal use of concrete and his speculative reconstructions and interpretations. His work may have dismayed fellow archaeologists but for the casual visitor, it evokes the splendour of the palace, and facilitates the interpretation of all the Minoan sites.

Site Tour

Raised walkways have been erected around most of the site to protect it from the wear and tear of countless tourists (in summer up to 4,000 come here daily). Visitors enter by the west court, then follow the walkway to the Corridor of the Procession, with a copy of the original fresco of a procession of over 500 figures. Steps lead up to the *piano nobile*, completely reconstructed by Evans and displaying reproductions of the palace's most famous frescoes. From here there are good views over the store-rooms and *pithoi* (large storage jars). The terrace steps lead down to the Central Court, formerly used for religious rituals and bull-leaping displays. In the northwest corner the throne room contains the original 'Throne of Minos' and a lustral basin (sunken bath) for purification. The seat in the antechamber is a reproduction of Minos' throne. On the far side of the central court the grand staircase (closed for restoration) leads down to what Evans believed to be the royal apartments: The Hall of the Double Axes, the King's Megaron and the most elaborately decorated of all the rooms, the Queen's Megaron. This was decorated with the well-known leaping dolphin fresco, and equipped with a bathroom and a lavatory with drains. The walkway continues round to the north entrance with its repro-duction of the Charging Bull fresco, and the theatre and Royal Road, said to be the oldest paved road in Europe.

A pithoi, *or large storage jar, used for palace supplies. Over 100 were discovered at Knosós*

The restored north entrance of the palace, which is decorated with a copy of the charging bull fresco

8
Moní Arkadíou

 28C2

 24km southeast of Réthymno

☎ (28310) 83116

🕐 Daily 8–8

🍴 Snack bar (£) on the premises, taverna (£) at Amnátos (4km north)

🚌 4 buses a day from Réthymno

♿ Access to monastery only

✋ Inexpensive

The mass suicide within Moní Arkadíou came to symbolise Cretan heroism and strengthened the Cretan struggle against the Turkish yoke.

The fame of Moní Arkadíou lies not so much in its splendid setting on a plateau in the Ída Mountains, nor in its beautiful baroque façade, but in the historic role it played during the struggle for freedom from Turkish rule in the 19th century. Isolated in the mountains, the monastery became an important centre of Cretan resistance, supporting uprisings against foreign powers.

On 9 November 1866, following a two-day siege, thousands of Turkish troops forced entry through the western gateway. Within the monastery hundreds of resistance fighters were taking refuge with their wives and children. Rather than suffer death at the hands of the Turks, the Cretans blew themselves up, so the story is told, by setting light to the powder magazine. Most of the Cretans within the monastery were killed, but so were hundreds of Turks – the exact number of deaths is unknown. Following the event many prominent figures in Europe rallied to support the Cretan cause, among them Garibaldi and Victor Hugo. Nearly a century later the writer Níkos Kazantzákis (► 14) retold the historic event in his powerful novel, *Freedom and Death*.

Visitors to the monastery can see the richly carved Venetian façade, dating from 1587, the restored interior of the church, the roofless powder magazine bearing scars of the explosion, and a small museum of icons, vessels and siege memorabilia. Close to the entrance to the monastery an ossuary containing the skulls of the siege victims is a chilling reminder of the events of 1866.

The elaborately carved façade of Moní Arkadíou

9
Moní Préveli

The peaceful setting overlooking the southern sea and the monastery's historic past combine to make Préveli one of Crete's most compelling sights.

When Crete fell to the Turks in the 17th century, the monks of Préveli decided to abandon their original monastery in favour of a more secluded location. Their new monastery, perched above the Libyan Sea, soon became a centre of resistance and grew wealthy on the olive groves, sheep, goats, wine, corn and other gifts that were bequeathed by Cretans who feared their possessions would otherwise fall into Turkish hands.

More recently the monastery sheltered Allied troops after the fall of Crete to the Germans in 1941, and assisted their evacuation from neighbouring beaches to the Egyptian port of Alexandria.

Largely rebuilt in 1835, then partially destroyed by the

➕ 28C2

✉ 13km east of Plakiás

☎ (28320) 31246

🕐 Daily 8–1:30, 3:30–8

🍴 Snack bar (£) on premises in summer

🚌 Limited bus service from Réthymno

♿ Possible for wheelchairs

✋ Moderate

↔ Préveli Beach (➤ 70), Plakiás (➤ 70)

Germans in reprisal for the protection of the soldiers, the monastery retains none of its original buildings, but it is nevertheless a handsome complex with splendid views.

The finest feature is the Church of Ágios Ioánnis (St John), a 19th-century reconstruction of the original 17th-century church, containing an elaborate inconostasis with many old icons and a gold cross with diamonds, containing what is said to be a fragment of the True Cross. The story goes that the Germans tried three times to steal the cross but each time they tried to start their escape aircraft, the engines failed. A small museum within the church houses vestments, silverware, icons and votive offerings.

The church and remains of the original monastery, Káto Moní Préveli, can still be seen beside the Megapótomos River, 3km inland.

Above: *street leading to Moní Préveli*
Below: *one way of getting around the island*

10
Panagía Kerá

The beautifully restored Byzantine frescoes adorning the walls and domes of this tiny church are remarkable for their realism and drama.

✝ 29E2

✉ Kritsá, 10km southwest of Ágios Nikólaos

☎ (28410) 51711

🕐 Daily 8:30–3

🍴 Cafés on premises (£), Paradise Restaurant across the road (££)

🚌 Regular service from Ágios Nikólaos

♿ Few

✋ Moderate

↔ Kritsá (► 53)

❓ Icons and guides for sale at shop

Panagía Kerá contains the finest examples of Byzantine art on the island

Set amid the olive and cypress trees of the Kritsá plain, this delightful little church dates back to the 13th and 14th centuries, and is a treasure house of religious art. Triangular buttresses supporting the aisles give the church an unusual appearance, but it is the interior, with the most complete series of Byzantine frescoes in Crete, that draws the crowds (arrive as early as possible to avoid the crush).

The only light in the church comes through the narrow apsidal windows and it takes time to decipher the different scenes. The very oldest frescoes are those of the apse, followed by the scenes from the Life of Christ in the dome and nave. More easily recognisable are the nave scenes of *The Nativity*, *Herod's Banquet* and *The Last Supper*.

The later wall paintings of the south and north aisles show a marked move towards naturalism. In the south aisle (where you enter) the scenes from the life of St Anne and of the Virgin Mary are lively 14th-century frescoes, the faces full of expression. Note the face of Anne, whose portrait dominates the apse, and the touching scene in the aisle of Mary looking dejected over Joseph's misunderstood reaction to her conception. An angel descends to explain to Joseph. The north aisle frescoes portray scenes of the *Last Judgement*, depictions of St Anthony and other saints, and a portrait of the founder of the church with his wife and daughter.

What to See

Above: *a pieced-together pithoi among the ruins
at Mália's archaeological site*
Right: *replica of a figure from the Procession
Fresco, Knosós*

27

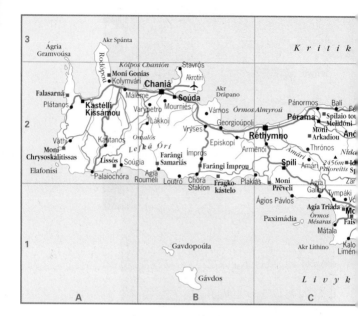

	A	B	C
3	Ágria Gramvoúsa · Akr Spánta · Rodópou · Kólpos Chaníon · Moní Goniás · Kolymvári · Chaniá · Stavrós · Akrotíri		Kritik
2	Falasarná · Plátanos · Kastélli Kissámou · Váthi · Moní Chrysoskalítissas · Kámnos · Omalós · Lissós · Elafonísi	Máleme · Varypetro · Lákkoi · Lefká Óri · Farángi Samariás · Soúgia · Ágia Roúmeli · Loutró · Chóra Sfakíon	Akr Drápano · Vámos · Mourniés · Vrýses · Episkopí · Ímpros · Farángi Ímprou · Fragko kástelo · Plakiás
1		Gavdopoúla · Gávdos	Ágios Pávlos · Paximádia · Akr Líthino · Livyk

Views across the gorse-covered hills to the sweeping beach of Falásarna on the west coast

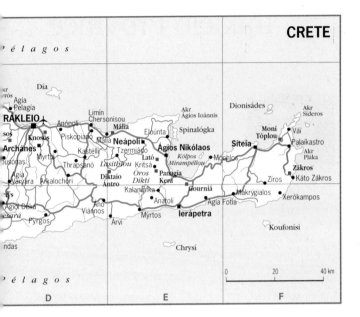

CRETE

Pélagos

Día

Akr
rós
Agía
Pelagia

RAKLEIO

Anópoli

Limín
Chersonísou

Akr
Ágios Ioánnis

Dionisádes

Akr
Sideros

sos
Knosós

Piskopianó

Mália

Moní
Tóplou

Vái

Palaikastro

Archánes

Myrtiá

Kastélli

Mália
Neápoli

Eloúnta

Spinalógka

Siteía

Akr
Pláka

usónas
Agía
Varvára
Arkalochóri

Thrapsanó

Tzermiádo

Lasíthiou

Lató

Ágios Nikólaos

Kólpos
Mirampéllou

Móchlos

Zákros

Káto Zákros

ýs
Ágioi Déka
esará

Diktaío
Ántro

Óros
Díkti

Panagía
Kerá

Zíros

Pyrgos

Ano
Viánnos

Kalamáfka

Gourniá

Makrygialos

Xerókampos

ndas

Anatolí

Myrtos

Ierápetra

Agía Fotiá

Árvi

Koufonísi

Chrysí

Pélagos

0   20   40 km

D   E   F

Irákleio Province

In the centre of the island, Irákleio is the most visited of all the provinces. Not only does it embrace the four great Minoan sites at Knosós, Faistós, Mália and Agía Triáda, but in Limín Chersonísou and Mália it also has the two biggest resorts on Crete. Irákleio itself is a bustling, traffic-ridden city but this should not deter sightseers from a visit to the Archaeological Museum, which houses the world's greatest collection of Minoan artefacts. Few tourists actually stay in the city, most preferring the beach resorts to the east. While the north coast has a long ribbon of tourist development, the south coast is far less accessible, with just a handful of small resorts. Of these, the one-time hippie haunt of Mátala, with a fine beach and rock caves, is the most developed.

> *'The people of Crete*
> *unfortunately make more*
> *history than they can*
> *consume locally.'*

SAKI
The Jesting of Arlington
Stringham (1914)

●

Above: *distinctive Cretan shuttered windows*

Irákleio

Fifth largest city in Greece, Irákleio is the capital of Crete and the commercial and cultural hub of the island. Herakleium to the Romans, Rabdh-el-Khandak (Castle of the Ditch) to the Saracens, Candia to the Venetians, Megélo Kástro (Great Fortress) to the Turks, it finally reverted to Herákleion (or Irákleio) in 1923. Badly damaged by bombs during World War II, it is today an essentially modern city.

Once a dusty town with an eastern flavour, Irákleio is now taking on a cosmopolitan air. Fashionable young people fill the cafés and smart boutiques sell the latest designs.

Everything of cultural interest lies conveniently within the ramparts and can easily be covered on foot. The most colourful quarter is the harbour, where fishermen gut their catch and skinny cats sniff around for titbits. The fortress overlooking the harbour and the nearby vaults of the arsenals are prominent reminders of the city's Venetian heyday. In the central Plateía Venizélos, cafés cluster around the fountain. From here the pedestrianised Odós Daidálos, lined with shops and tavernas, leads on to the huge Plateía Elefthérias and the famous Archaeological Museum (► 17–18).

Most of the architecture is postwar, but there are a number of old ruins or fountains, often incorporated into modern buildings and some neo-classical buidings. The Venetian walls, 40m thick in places, were constructed in 1462 on earlier Byzantine foundations, and extended in 1538. Most of the gates survive, and it is possible to walk along the line of the walls for about 4km, though only 1km of the walk is actually on top of the walls. Near here, is the tomb of Nikos Kazantzákis – Crete's most famous writer.

Above: the Venetian lion of St Mark guards the fortress
Below: fishing boats in the old harbour

What to See in Irákleio

AGÍA AIKATERINÍ (MUSEUM OF RELIGIOUS ART)   ✪✪✪

✝ 36B2
✉ Plateía Aikaterinis
☎ (2810) 288825
🕐 Mon–Sat 9:30–2:30, Tue, Thu, Fri also 4:30–6:30; Jan and Dec, mornings only
🍴 Cafés (£) in Plateía Aikaterinis
♿ 2 shallow steps, otherwise no problem
✋ Moderate

Within the Church of Agía Aikateriní (St Catherine), the Museum of Religious Art houses the most important collection of icons in Crete. During the 16th and 17th centuries the church was part of the Mount Sinai Monastery School, which became one of the centres of the 'Cretan Renaissance'. The style of painting was characterised by the intermingling of Byzantine iconography with elements inspired by the Western Renaissance. One of the pupils here was Mikhaíl Damaskinós, and the six icons by him, on the right as you go in, are the finest works of art in the museum. Doménico Theotokópoulos, more commonly known as El Greco (▶ 14), may have been one of his contemporaries here.

ARCHAEOLOGICAL MUSEUM (▶ 17–18, TOP TEN)

ÁGIOS MÁRCOS   ✪

Below: the Church of Ágios Márcos was formerly the burial place of the Dukes of Crete

✝ 36B2
✉ Odós 25 Avgoústou
☎ (2810) 399228
🕐 Daily 9–1 and some evenings
🍴 Cafés and restaurants (£–££) nearby
♿ Few
✋ Free
↔ Morozíni Fountain (▶ 35)

The Basilica of St Mark, fronted by an arcaded portico, was built in 1239 by the Venetians and dedicated to their patron saint. The first church was destroyed by an earthquake in 1303 and its successor followed the same fate in 1508, but it was rebuilt and, like many others on Crete, became a mosque under the Turks. It later fell into decline but was restored in 1956–61 and today serves as an exhibition hall. Look out for the marble doorway inside, which is decorated with bunches of grapes.

View over the town from the Venetian walls; and (inset) the church of Ágios Títos

ÁGIOS PÉTROS ✪

Just to the northeast of the Historical Museum of Crete, the evocative ruins and arches of Ágios Pétros lie between the sea and graffiti-splattered modern buildings. The church was built by Dominican monks in the first half of the 13th century and converted into the mosque of Sultan Ibrahim under the Turks. The southern chapel preserves the only 15th-century frescoes in Irákleio, but the church is currently undergoing restoration and is temporarily closed to the public.

✚ 36B3
✉ Odós Sofokli Venizélou
☎ None
🕐 Currently closed to the public
↔ Historical Museum of Crete (► 34)

ÁGIOS TÍTOS ✪

Named after the saint who was sent by St Paul to convert the Cretans to Christianity, this building has had a chequered history. The Byzantine church was rebuilt several times after earthquakes, converted into a mosque by the Turks, ruined by another earthquake in 1856, rebuilt again, and, in 1923, reconsecrated to St Titus. The chapel to the left, by the entrance, houses a gold reliquary chalice containing the head of St Titus. This precious relic was taken to Venice for safekeeping when Irákleio fell to the Turks; it was finally returned to its rightful home in 1966 – 300 years later.

✚ 36C2
✉ Odós 25 Avgoústou
☎ (2810) 346221
🕐 Mon–Sat 8–12, 5–7
🍴 Cafés and restaurants (£–££) on Plateía Ágiou Titou
♿ Few
🎟 Free
↔ Ágios Márcos (► 32), Morozíni Fountain (► 35)

ISTORIKÓ MOUSEÍO KRÍTIS ✪✪✪
(HISTORICAL MUSEUM OF CRETE)

This museum takes up the story where the Archaeological Museum (➤ 17–18) leaves off and provides a fascinating insight into the island's turbulent history, from the early Christian era to the 20th century. Slightly away from the city centre, the museum is free from the crowding that you find at the Archaeological Museum and is therefore very pleasant to explore.

The collection starts with an exhibition of artefacts from the Christian period, with emphasis on the Venetian occupation and the Cretan War (1645–1669). This is illustrated by plans, photographs, clear explanations and a highly detailed model of Candia (Irákleio) in 1645. On the same floor the Ceramics Room illustrates the way in which pottery has evolved over 15 centuries.

The Medieval and Renaissance section displays Byzantine, Venetian and Turkish sculpture, Cretan-school icons, coins, jewellery and a collection of copies of Byzantine frescoes from Cretan churches. An early painting by El Greco (➤ 14) depicts a stormy *View of Mount Sinai* (c1570), with tiny figures of pilgrims climbing up the craggy peak to the Monastery of St Catherine.

The struggle for Cretan independence and the period of autonomy (1898–1908) is illustrated by portraits of revolutionaries, flags, weapons and photographs. The reconstructions of the studies of the writer Níkos Kazantzákis (➤ 14) and Emmanuel Tsouderós, Greek Prime Minister at the time of the Battle of Crete, bring you into the 20th century. The folk rooms on the fourth floor display local crafts and contain a replica of a traditional village home.

🔒 36B3
✉ Lysimáchou Kalokairinoú 7
☎ (2810) 283219
🕐 Mon–Fri 9–5, Sat 9–2
🍴 Waterfront restaurants nearby (£–££)
♿ Only the first floor accessible for wheelchairs
💷 Moderate
↔ Koúles Fortress (➤ 35)

Above: *portrait of Manolis Kazanis, a local leader during the 1821 War of Independence, in the Historical Museum*

Below: *traditional Cretan interior in the Historical Museum*

KOÚLES FORTRESS ✪✪✪

Guarding the harbour, this mighty fortress was built by the Venetians in the 16th century on the foundations of an earlier fort. Various strongholds had occupied the site since the Saracens arrived in the 9th century, but none as huge and impregnable as the Venetian structure. Called Rocca al Mare by the Venetians, it resisted the Turks for 21 years, finally surrendering in 1669. The winged lion of St Mark – symbol of Venice – decorates three sides of the fort, the best preserved on the far, seaward side.

There is little to see inside the fort, but the cool chambers and the walk along the causeway beyond the fortress provide welcome respite from the bustle of the town. From the top there are fine views of the harbour, town and the towering peaks of the Psiloreítis in the distance. Clearly visible across the street from the harbour are the vaulted chambers of the *Arsenali*, where the Venetian war galleys were built and repaired. The shipyards were built between the 13th and the 17th centuries.

🕂 36C3
✉ Irákleio Harbour
☎ (2810) 288484
🕐 Mon–Fri 8–6, Sat–Sun 10–5
🍴 Tavernas near the harbour (£–£££)
♿ None
💷 Moderate
↔ Historical Museum of Crete (➤ 34)
❓ Opening hours change when there are temporary exhibitions here. Upper storey used as an open-air theatre in summer

MOROZÍNI FOUNTAIN ✪✪✪

The central feature of Plateía Venizélos, the fountain was built in 1628 by Francesco Morozini, Venetian Governor of the island. A 16km-long aqueduct was built to channel water to it from Mount Gioúchtas in the south. The fountain, which is rarely in action, has eight circular basins, decorated with reliefs of nymphs, tritons, dolphins, mermaids, cherubs and mythical creatures. Above, the 14th-century carved lions were incorporated into the fountain and formerly supported a statue of Neptune. Plateía Venizélos (familiarly known as Fountain Square) is the tourist centre of Irákleio, and is packed with bustling cafés and restaurants.

🕂 36B2
✉ Plateía Venizélos
🍴 Cafés and restaurants (£–££)
↔ Ágios Títos (➤ 33), Ágios Márcos (➤ 32)

NATURAL HISTORY MUSEUM ✪✪

Crete's wildlife, plants and landscape are attractively presented in this museum, set in a modern building outside the city walls on the road to Knosós. If you are planning a trip to the countryside or a drive around the island it will certainly enhance your appreciation of the things you will see. Life-sized dioramas on the ground floor re-create the island's flora and fauna in their natural habitats. Displays highlight birdlife and endangered species such as the Cretan wild goat, or *kri-kri*, which can still be seen in areas of Crete such as the Samaria Gorge. Glass cases in the gift shop house live snakes, the curious ocellated skink and the Cretan spiny mouse. The botanical garden is filled with aromatic wild herbs, while upstairs exhibits focus on the island's geological and human evolution.

The Morozíni Fountain

🕂 Off the map 29C1
✉ Odós Knosuou 157
☎ (2810) 324711
🕐 Daily 9–7
🍴 Coffee shop on site (£)
🚌 2, 3, 4 from Irákleio
💷 Free

35

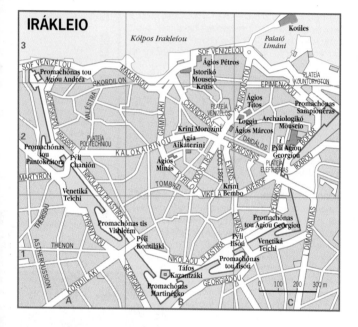

The imposing Bethlehem Bastion forming part of a semi-circle of medieval city walls

Around Irákleio

Start at Plateía Eleuthérias (Freedom Square), a traffic-encircled hub of the city with gardens and cafés.

North of the square visit Irákleio's famous Archaeological Museum (➤ 17–18).

West of Plateía Eleuthérias take Odós Daidálos, a pedestrian shopping thoroughfare leading to Plateía Venizélos, the heart of the city.

Try *bougátsa*, a pastry speciality, in one of the cafés overlooking the Morozíni Fountain (➤ 35).

Facing Odós Daidálos, turn right and make for the market (➤ 106) in Odós 1866 on the far side of the crossroads.

In the square at the end of the street a café occupies a hexagonal building which was formerly a Turkish fountain; the nearby Venetian Bembo fountain (1588) was assembled with a headless Roman statue and other antiquities.

Returning along Odós 1866, take the second street on your left, and at the end turn right and then left over Odós 1821 to bring you into Plateía Aikaterínis.

The square is dominated by the huge neo-Byzantine Cathedral of Ágios Minás (1895). In its shadow lies the original, more charming Ágios Minás, with a splendid iconostatis. On the near side, Agía Aikateriní houses a fine collection of icons (➤ 32).

Turn right off the square for the busy Odós Kalokairinou and right again. A left turn at the crossroads will bring you back to the Morozíni Fountain. Cross the square for Odós 25 Avgoústou.

On the right is Ágios Márcos (St Mark ➤ 32); further on the reconstructed arcaded Loggia (today the Town Hall) was the meeting-place for Venetian nobility. Just beyond lies Ágios Títos (➤ 33) on its own square.

Continue down the street for the harbour and Venetian fortress (➤ 35).

Distance
3km

Time
2–5 hours depending on visits

Start Point
Plateía Eleftherías
✚ 36C2

End Point
Harbour
✚ 36C3

Lunch
Ippokambos (£)
✉ Odós Sófokli Venizélou
☎ (2810) 280240

The neo-Byzantine Cathedral of Agíos Minás has a sumptuous interior

What to See in Irákleio Province

AGÍA PELAGÍA ✪

Rather more stylish than most of the other north coast resorts, Agía Pelagía enjoys a beautiful hill setting, overlooking a bay of deep blue water. Buses link it to Irákleio but many guests prefer to stay put, enjoying the beach, the clear, calm waters, the watersports and the handful of bars and tavernas which provide simple evening entertainment. The setting and proximity to Irákleio are attracting an increasing amount of tourism and the village is currently growing apace.

AGÍA TRIÁDA (➤ 16, TOP TEN)

FAISTÓS (➤ 19, TOP TEN)

FÓDELE ✪✪

Fódele is the birthplace of El Greco (➤ 14) – or at least it claims to be. Scholars now argue that the painter was born in Irákleio. But in any event the village makes a very pleasant detour from the main highway, along a verdant valley of orange and lemon groves. Along the main village road ladies sell linen, lace and embroidery and there are simple stalls selling citrus fruits.

Over the bridge the village is less commercialised, with delightful streets lined by rustic, flower-decked dwellings. The **El Greco House** is well signed, and lies about 1km from the centre, opposite the Byzantine Church of the Panagía.

➕ 29D2
✉ 18km northwest of Irákleio
🍴 Beach tavernas (£–££)
🚍 Regular service to Irákleio
♿ None
↔ Fódele (➤ below)

Above: *the Church of the Panagía at Fódele and (inset) a village lace seller*

➕ 28C2
✉ 19km northwest of Irákleio, 3km south of the E75
🍴 Taverna El Greco (£)
🚍 2 per day from Irákleio
♿ None
↔ Agía Pelagía (above)

Smiti El Greco (El Greco House)
☎ 2810) 521500
🕐 Tue–Sun 9–5
 Inexpensive

GÓRTYS (► 21, TOP TEN)

KNOSÓS (► 22, TOP TEN)

LIMÍN CHERSONÍSOU
Packed with holidaymakers
in pursuit of fun and sun,
Limín Chersonísou and
neighbouring Mália make
up the biggest tourist development on Crete. The strips
of grey sand and pebble are

Did you know ?

*According to one of the many legends, Ariadne,
daughter of King Minos who helped Theseus to
escape the Labyrinth after slaying the Minotaur,
was killed on the island of Diá. Today the island,
which can be visited by boat, is home to the rare
Cretan ibex, but a quiet sanctuary it is not.
Diá lies directly under the airport flight path!*

barely sufficient to cope with the crowds, but many
visitors opt to spend long hours in sea-view bars anyway.
Nightlife centres on the discos, clubs and bars, some of
which operate all night long.

A walk around the harbour provides a pleasant break
from the bustle as well as fine views of the mountains
towering behind the high-rise blocks. A seaport thrived
here in ancient times but only vestiges survive of its
ancient splendour. The submerged remains of the Roman
harbour are just visible off the headland and, amid the
video bars, souvenirs and boutiques on the seafront, you
can see the fenced-in fragments of a fish mosaic which
was originally part of a Roman fountain.

The resort offers a variety of nearby diversions. The
Lychnostatis (Cretan Open-Air Museum ► 110) gives an
insight into authentic Cretan life. At Piskopianó's **Museum
of Rural Life** workshops and agricultural tools are
displayed within an old olive-oil mill. To the east and south
of the resort, explore the slides and rides of the Star Water
Park and the Aqua Splash Water Park (► 110).

✚ 29D2
⊠ 28km east of Irákleio
🚌 Regular buses from
   Irákleio
🍴 Countless bars and
   tavernas in the centre
   (£–££)
↔ Mália (► 40), Star Water
   Park and Aqua Splash
   Water Park (► 110),
   Cretan Open-Air
   Museum (► 110)

**Agrotileo Mouseio Limín
Chersonísou
(Museum of Rural Life)**
⊠ Piskopianó (3km south of
   Limín Chersonísou)
☎ (28970) 23303
🕐 Apr–Oct daily 11–1, 4–8
♿ Wheelchair access

*Limín Chersonísou is Crete's largest package
holiday resort*

39

29E2

✉ 36km east of Irákleio

🍴 Large choice in the centre (£–££)

🚌 Regular service from Irákleio

♿ Few

↔ Limín Chersonísou (► 39)

Anakforo Mália (Mália Palace)

 29E2

✉ 3km east of Mália

☎ (28970) 31597

🕐 Daily 8:30–3. Closed Mon from Nov–Mar

🍴 Café/bar on premises; restaurants (£–££) in Mália (3km)

🚌 Regular service from Mália and Irákleio

♿ One of the few Minoan sites accessible by wheelchair

🎫 Moderate; free on Sun in winter

The long, sandy beach of Mália is normally packed with holidaymakers

MÁLIA ✪✪✪

To the east of this resort lie the ancient Minoan remains of **Mália Palace**. The ruins are not as spectacular as those of Knosós, but the setting, on a quiet stretch of the coast between the sea and Lasíthiou mountains, is rather more impressive. Those who have visited Knosós or Faistós will recognise the layout around the central court, with store-rooms, ceremonial stairways, royal apartments and lustral basin. The origins are similar too. The palace was built in around 1900 BC but destroyed by an earthquake in 1700 BC. A second palace was built on the foundations, but (unlike Knosós) it was completely destroyed in the unknown catastrophe of 1450 BC. Among the many treasures discovered here were an axe head in the shape of a leopard and a sword with a crystal hilt, both of which are now in the Archaeological Museum, Irákleio (► 17–18).

French archaeologists are continuing to excavate a town which lay to the north and west of the palace. A 10-minute walk northeast towards the sea brings you to the Khrysólakkos (Pit of Gold), a burial site where priceless jewellery was discovered, including an exquisite gold bee pendant, also in the Irákleio Museum.

The unashamedly brash and rowdy resort of Mália – along with neighbouring Limín Chersonísou (► 39) – is the party capital of the island. Packed with discos, video bars and burger joints, it is similar to Limín Chersonísou, but has a far better beach, with sands stretching a considerable distance to the east.

MÁTALA ⭐⭐

Mátala made its name in the 1960s when foreign hippies (Cat Stevens and Bob Dylan among them) took advantage of the free accommodation offered by the historic rock caves. Unpopular with both locals and archaeologists, the hippies were thrown out long ago. Today Mátala attracts tourists of all ages, but it still appeals in particular to independent travellers – especially off-season. The climate is milder than the north coast and spectacular sunsets can be enjoyed from the beach tavernas and bars, one of which, Lion's Bar, calls itself the Last Bar Before Africa – true if it wasn't for the island of Gávdos (► 84, 86).

Mátala's main attraction is its beautiful sand and shingle beach, sheltered between sloping ochre-coloured cliffs. Consisting of compacted, yellow earth, the cliffs are riddled with man-made caves, particularly along the promontory on the north side. The caves range from small hacked-out holes to entire rooms, complete with carved benches, steps, windows and fireplaces. No-one knows who made the original caves, but they are generally believed to have been Roman or early Christian tombs.

The sands are very crowded in summer. Behind the beach the village now caters almost entirely for tourists, with souvenirs and motorbike rental agencies, but the resort is still pleasantly free of high-rise buildings, much of the accommodation being in guest houses. There are boat trips to smaller beaches further south or you can walk over the rocks (about 20 minutes) to Red Beach, named after its reddish-brown sands.

+ 28C1
🖂 70km southwest of Irákleio
🕐 Caves 11:30–7
🍴 Cafés and tavernas (£–££) on the beach
🚌 Services from Irákleio, Moíres and Faistós
♿ None
🅿 Caves moderate
↔ Faistós (► 19), Agía Triáda (► 16), Museum of Cretan Ethnology at Vóroi (► 43)

Above: *Mátala is a small but highly popular tourist resort*
Below: *people once lived in the rock-cut tombs in the cliffs*

+ 29D2
☒ 16km southeast of
Irákleio
🍴 Cafés and tavernas (£) on
the square

Níkos Kazantzákis Museum
☎ (2810) 742451
🕐 Mar–Oct Mon–Sat 9–1
(also Mon, Wed, Sat, Sun
4–8); Nov–Feb Sun 9–2
♿ Few
💷 Moderate
↔ Knosós (▶ 22)

+ 29D2
☒ 10km west of Irákleio
☎ (2810) 831372
🕐 Daily 8:30–3
🍴 Taverna (£) next to the
site
🚌 Service from Irákleio
♿ None
💷 Moderate; free on Sun in
winter

Right: *ruins at peaceful
Tílisos, site of three large
Minoan villas*

MYRTÍA ✪

Myrtía is a pretty place to visit, surrounded by vines and full of flowers and potted plants. It is proud of its Kazantzákis connection, and announces the museum at either end of the village in five languages. Níkos Kazantzákis' father lived on the central square in a large house which has been converted into a **museum** dedicated to the writer. Best known for his novel, *Zorba the Greek*, Kazantzákis was also a poet, travel journalist and essayist (▶ 14). The museum houses a collection of first editions of his books, costumes from his plays, stills from films of his books, photographs and personal belongings.

TÍLISOS ✪✪

Reached off the old Irákleio/Réthymno national road, and set in the mountains, surrounded by olive groves and vineyards, Tílisos is home to three Minoan villas dating from the New Palace period (1700–1450 BC). Like Knosós and Faistós, which were built at the same time, there are signs of earlier structures. Excavated in the 20th century, the villas are referred to as Houses A, B and C, the best preserved being A (straight ahead as you enter the site) and C (the house on the left).

The ruins are far less imposing than those of the famous Minoan palaces, but it is interesting to see where lesser mortals lived – it is also a delightful, peaceful spot for a stroll. House A, largest of the villas, has storerooms with reconstructed *pithoi* (large storage jars), a court with columns, a lustral basin and stairs which indicate an upper floor. House C is the most elaborate of the three.

Did you know ?

In around 1450 BC Crete was the victim of a sudden disaster. With the exception of Knosós, the Minoan palaces were burned down and other settlements destroyed. The cause of the catastrophe remains a mystery, but among various theories put forward are the volcanic eruption of Théra (Santorini), a catastrophic earthquake or an attack by invaders.

VÓROI ⭐⭐⭐

The old village of Vóroi was put on the tourist map in 1985 when it became the home of the excellent **Mouseío Kritikis Ethnologia (Museum of Cretan Ethnology)**. In 1992 a further boost came with the award of Best European Museum by the Council of Europe. Inconspicuously located in a building near the church, it is a modern museum with exhibits beautifully laid out behind glass and informatively labelled. Devoted to traditional crafts and ways of life in rural Crete, the museum has separate sections dealing with food and diet, agriculture, weaving, pottery, metalwork, transportation and religion. The first section shows plants and other edibles with which Cretans used to supplement their meagre diets, and many of them are still used today, such as the group of wild plants called *Chorta* and the aromatic plants for infusions.

The weaving section displays 25 different types of baskets made of reed, wild olive, rush, myrtle and other natural materials. The baskets served a variety of purposes, from trapping fish, harvesting sultana grapes and keeping snails to draining cheese. Pottery, made in Crete since Minoan times, includes vessels for *rakí*, vinegar and water, and storage pots for oil, wine, cereals and honey.

28C1
4km north of Faistós
Tavernas (£–££)
Service from Irákleio

Museum of Cretan Ethnology
28C1
(28920) 91112
Apr–Oct daily 10–6; in winter by appointment
(28920) 91110

Below: *detail from the Museum of Cretan Ethnology*
Bottom: *the village church*

None 43

Lasíthiou

This eastern province may not boast the majestic mountains of central or western Crete, but it has plenty of other attractions, both scenic and cultural. The tourist mecca is Ágios Nikólaos, overlooking the beautiful Gulf of Mirampéllou.  From here the main road snakes its way to Siteía, hub of the eastern end of Crete and a base for the beaches of Vái and Ítanos. Further south lie the ancient remains of the palace of Zákros, one of the major Minoan sites on the island. The most dramatic geographical feature of the region is the Lasíthiou Plateau, whose flat, fertile fields are ringed by the towering peaks of the Díkti Mountains. The south coast, where plastic greenhouses proliferate, is less scenic than the north, with little development. Ierápetra, the main town, has limited attractions for tourists.

> '*No mortal could vie with Zeus, for his mansions and his possessions are deathless.*'
>
> HOMER
> *The Odyssey* (c700 BC)

Left: *the pretty resort of Agíos Nikólaos, tourist hub of eastern Crete*
Above: *the sails of a stone windmill, symbol of the Lasíthiou Plateau*

What to See in Lasíthiou

ÁGIOS NIKÓLAOS ✪✪✪

From a peaceful little harbour town, Ágios Nikólaos (or 'Ag Nik' as English-speaking regulars like to call it) has grown into the most popular resort on Crete. In the Hellenistic era this was the port for Lató, whose archaeological remains can be seen in the hills to the west (▶ 54). The town fell into decline under the Romans but was later developed by the Venetians, who built a fort dominating the Bay of Mirampéllou (Beautiful View). In 1303 this was damaged by an earthquake, then later razed to the ground by the Turks. In 1870 Sfakiots from western Crete settled at the port, naming it after the Byzantine church of Ágios Nikólaos to the north. The town today may not boast the architectural features and historic background of Crete's other regional capitals; nonetheless it is a very picturesque resort with a lively atmosphere that appeals to all ages. There is nothing particularly Cretan about it, and the chief attraction is, and always has been, the setting on a hilly promontory overlooking the deep blue Gulf of Mirampéllou.

In the centre of the resort tavernas and cafés cluster around the busy fishing harbour and the deep-water Lake Voulisméni, which is linked to the harbour by a short canal. By day the main activity is strolling around the quaysides, browsing at souvenirs and whiling away the hours over leisurely lunches. Evening life centres on bars with music, cafés with cocktails and half a dozen discos. Luxury hotels provide pristine beaches, but public bathing areas leave much to be desired. The small strips of shingle and rock are invariably crowded, but you can walk or take a bus to the sandy beach of Almirós, 2km to the south.

A steep walk up from the port leads to the Archaiologikó Mouseío (Archaeological Museum). Dating from the 1970s this is a modern museum with a small collection of locally found treasures that were previously housed in the Archaeological Museum in Irákleio, and it is well worth a visit. Exhibits are arranged chronologically,

 29E2

🍴 Harbour cafés and tavernas (£–£££)

🚌 Regular service to Irákleio, Mália, Limín Chersonísou, Siteía and Ierápetra

🚢 Services to Siteía, Piraeus, Milos, Santoríni, Karpathos, Kassos, Kas, Rhodes and other islands, mainly in summer

ℹ️ Odós Akti I Koundourou 20 ☎ (284101) 22357

♿ Few

↔️ Panagía Kerá (▶ 26), Lató (▶ 54)

Archaeological Museum

✉️ Odós Palaioĺogou 68

☎ (28410) 24943

🕐 Tue–Sun 8:30–3

🍴 Taverna Aouas (££)

♿ Possible for wheelchairs

💷 Moderate; free on Sun and national hols from Nov–Mar

from the early Minoan and neolithic period (6000–2100 BC) to the Graeco-Roman era. The emphasis is on Minoan works of art including terracotta figures of deities, Vasilikí flameware vases, seal stones, pottery and jewellery. The prize piece is the early Minoan Goddess of Mirtos in Room II – a stylised, innovative libation vessel in the form of a clay figure (c2500 BC) with a fat body, long skinny neck and tiny head, clasping a water jug. In the same room the beautiful gold jewellery in the form of ribbons, leaves and flowers, came from the island off Móchlos (➤ 54). The late Minoan 'larnakes' or clay sarcophagi in the next room were also used as bath tubs – one of them still contains the bones of two bodies. In Room IV, a rare late Minoan infant burial tomb is displayed exactly as it was found by the excavators. In the last room the grinning 1st century AD skull, bearing a wreath of gold olive leaves, was discovered at the Potamós necropolis near Ágios Nikólaos. The silver coin found in its mouth is the fare for the ferry ride to the Underworld, across the mythical River Styx.

The tiny **Mouseío Laographiko (Folk Museum)** close to the tourist office is devoted mainly to folk art. Among the displays of local crafts are finely woven and embroidered textiles, woodcarvings, weapons, ceramics and Byzantine icons. The collection of old photographs includes shots of 19th-century revolutionaries and depictions of Ágios Nikólaos at the beginning of the 20th century, showing how the port looked before the advent of tourism.

Left: *fishing boats along Lake Voulisméni*
Below left: *skull with wreath of gold olive leaves, at the Archaeological Museum, Agíos Nikólaos*

Folk Museum

🏛 29E2
✉ Ground floor of Harbour Master's Office, opposite the bridge
☎ (28410) 25093
🕐 Apr–Oct Sun–Fri 10–4
♿ Few
💰 Moderate

A narrow canal links Lake Voulisméni with the harbour

A Walk in Ágios Nikólaos

Distance
1.8km

Time
2 hours (including sights)

Start Point
Harbour
➕ 29E2

End Point
Lake Voulisméni
➕ 29E2

Lunch
Aouas Taverna (£.£)
✉ Odós Paleológou
☎ (28410) 23231

This walk begins at the harbour in the centre of the resort.

From the harbour walk up the tamarisk-lined Odós Roussou Koundoúrou, one of the two main shopping streets. Take the first street to the left, Odós Sfakianáki.

Towards the far end of Odós Sfakianáki there are splendid views of the Gulf of Mirampéllou. The marina below was constructed in 1994.

At the end of the street, turn left to climb some steps, then make your way down to the waterfront. Here, turn left, passing Kitroplatía Beach, and continue along the waterfront until you come to the harbour.

Cafés and tavernas provide pretty views of the lake, but you pay for the privilege

Soak up the atmosphere of the harbour with a drink in one of the waterside cafés. The boats and cruisers moored here offer fishing, swimming and glass-bottom boat trips, excursions to Spinalókga Island, (➤ 51, 84) and evening tours of the bay.

Make for the bridge on the west corner of the harbour and the small Folk Museum (➤ 47). Walk up the steep Odós Palaiológou for a visit to the Archaeological Museum (➤ 46), then retrace your steps down to the lake on your right.

The 64m-deep Lake Voulisméni, encircled by fishing boats and flanked by cliffs on its western side, was originally believed to be bottomless. In 1867 it was linked to the harbour by a channel and cleared of its stagnant waters. Today it is a tourist magnet, the lakeview cafés luring customers with their tempting range of exotic ices and cocktails. For the best views take the steps up at the far side, beyond the Café du Lac.

DIKTAÍO ÁNTRO (DÍKTAEAN CAVE) ✪✪

According to myth, the Díktaean Cave was the birthplace of Zeus. His father, Kronos, who feared being overthrown by a son, consumed the first five of his offspring. However, when Zeus was born, his mother Rhea presented Kronos with a stone instead of a baby and Zeus was concealed inside the cave, protected by warriors and fed by a goat. As a small child, he was then transferred to the Ídaean Cave (➤ 69).

The actual cave is impressive, but the site is highly commercialised and crowded. Beware of greedy car park attendants, costly donkey rides and persistent guides. Non-slippery shoes are essential. There are now concrete steps and lighting to help you negotiate the 65-m descent, but unless you are hiring a guide you may want to bring a torch to better examine the cave's natural features more closely.

The cave is a kilometre up from the car park, via a steep, stepped path. An expensive donkey ride is the easy alternative. If you happen to arrive before the tour crowds, the dark cave, with its stalactites and stalagmites, is highly atmospheric. Down in the depths, the venue of ancient cult ceremonies, guides point out the chamber where Zeus was born, and features such as the face of Kronos and a stalagmite in the shape of Rhea and Zeus. Altars, idols and a large number of pottery and bronze votive offerings were found within the cave, some dating back to a pre-Minoan era.

🔲 29E2
✉ Psychró, Lasíthiou
☎ (29770) 364335
🕐 Daily 8–7, 8:30–3 in winter
🍴 Tavernas (££) at the entrance, less commercialised ones in the village
🚌 Limited service from Irákleio and from Ágios Nikólaos
♿ None, highly unsuitable
💷 Expensive, particularly if you take a donkey and/or guide
↔ Lasíthiou Plateau (➤ 53)

The easiest way to the Díktaean Cave... but it's not too far by foot

🏛 29E2
✉ 7km north of Ágios Nikólaos
🍴 Cafés and restaurants (£–££) around the harbour
🚌 Regular service to Ágios Nikólaos
♿ None
↔ Ágios Nikólaos (➤ 46)
❓ Boats to Spinalógka island daily in season, every 30 minutes 9–4:30

View of Eloúnta from the fortified islet of Spinalógka, and (inset) fishing boats at Eloúnta

ELOÚNTA AND SPINALÓGKA ✪✪

Thanks to a stunning setting and a choice of luxury hotels Eloúnta is one of Crete's most desirable resorts. It lies north of Ágios Nikólaos, reached by a road which snakes its way above the Gulf of Mirampéllou, then drops scenically down to the centre of the resort. Life here focuses on the cafés and tavernas around the boat-filled harbour, and the long sandy beach stretching beyond.

Coming into the resort from Ágios Nikólaos, a sharp right turning off the main road leads to a causeway linking Eloúnta to the Spinalógka peninsula. From here you can see the submerged remains of Venetian salt pans. The sunken remnants of the Graeco-Roman city state of Oloús lie towards the end of the causeway to the right of the peninsula. The remains are barely visible but the peninsula is a pleasant place to stroll, with coastal paths and birdlife.

A path beside the Canal Bar (just across the bridge) leads to a Byzantine mosaic featuring fish and geometric designs – this is all that remains of an early Christian basilica.

Eloúnta's luxury accommodation, including Crete's finest hotel (Eloúnta Beach ➤ 103) is situated away from the centre, off the road going south to Ágios Nikólaos. In peaceful surroundings, the hotels have their own private beaches and take full advantage of the glorious views over the gulf.

The rocky island of Spinalógka, reached by *caïque*, lies off shore and is dominated by its Venetian fortress, built in 1579 to protect the port of Eloúnta. A resistance movement operated here and it was not until 1715, 46 years after the Turkish conquest of the rest of Crete, that the fort finally surrendered. In 1903 the island was turned into a leper colony, where conditions were cruel and prison-like until the construction of a hospital in 1937. Twenty years later the colony was closed and the patients were taken to an Athens hospital. Today the island is uninhabited and the fortress and town are in ruins.

The ruins of workshops, storerooms and dwellings at the Minoan town of Gourniá

GOURNIÁ ✪✪✪

The ruins of the Minoan town of Gourniá sprawl over the hillside, just off the main Ágios Nikólaos–Siteía coastal road. The site is remarkably extensive, and the excavations revealed a thriving Minoan trading town of winding alleys lined by tiny houses, workshops, a marketplace and, on top of the hill, a palace, believed to have belonged to the local ruler or governor. The palace was originally three storeys high, with pillars, courtyards, storerooms and apartments. In relation to Knosós and Faistós this was something of a mini palace, and the people who lived in the town were probably quite humble in comparison to those of the more famous establishments. Like the other Minoan sites of Crete, Gourniá was destroyed in 1450 BC, then virtually abandoned. Many finds are housed in the Archaeological Museum in Irákleio (➤ 17, 18) and a few in the museum at Siteía (➤ 57). If the site is closed, there is a good view from the lay-by next to the entrance track.

➕ 29E2
✉ 19km southeast of Ágios Nikólaos
☎ (28410) 24943
🕐 Tue–Sun 8:30–3
🍴 Fish tavernas at Pachiá Ammos (£–££), 2km
🚌 Service to Ágios Nikólaos and Siteía
♿ None
💰 Moderate; free on Sun in winter
↔ Agios Nikólaos (➤ 46)

29E1

35km south of Ágios
Nikólaos

Regular service to Ágios
Nikólaos, Irákleio and
Siteía

Tavernas on the seafront
(£–££)

Few

Archaeological Museum

(28420) 28721

Tue–Sun 8:30–3

Moderate

IERÁPETRA ✪

Ierápetra is the most southerly town of Europe, enjoying mild winters and many months of sun, and even in mid-winter people bathe in the sea. Agriculture is the mainstay, with off-season vegetables produced in the ugly plastic greenhouses which surround the town.

Both a workaday town and tourist resort, Ierápetra has a bustling, slightly scruffy centre, a pleasant seafront promenade, a long grey sand beach and an old Turkish quarter with a mosque and fountain house. Architecturally it is uninspiring, and it has little to show of its past importance as a flourishing trading centre. Under the Dorians this was a leading city of Crete, and during the Roman occupation it saw the construction of temples, theatres and other fine buildings. Evidence of its more recent history is the Venetian fortress guarding the harbour. Built in 1212, and refortified by the Turks, this is used today for cultural events during July and August.

The **Archaiologikó Mouseío (Archaeological Museum)** in the centre has a small collection of local finds from Minoan to Roman times. They are not labelled or described, but an English-speaking custodian can usually help. The museum's showpiece is a Minoan *larnax*, or clay coffin, from Episkopí, north of Ierápetra, which is decorated with lively hunting scenes.

In high season boats leave from the quayside every morning for the island of Yaidhouronísi (or Chrýsi Island, ► 84) – a popular excursion for those who want to escape the bustle of the town.

Above: *the fortress at the harbourside of Ierápetra, rebuilt by the Venetians*

KRITSÁ VILLAGE ✪

Clinging to the slopes of the Díkti Mountains, Kritsá is a large hill village with fine views over the valley. Crafts are the speciality and shops are hung with rugs, embroidery and other homemade (and foreign) products. So close to Ágios Nikólaos and also home to the Panagía Kerá (► 26), this is a popular destination for tour coaches, but despite inevitable commercialism, the village retains much of its charm as a working hill community.

LASÍTHIOU PLATEAU ✪✪✪

The most visited inland region of Lasíthiou, the plateau has a spectacular setting, encircled by the Díktaean peaks. Watered by the melting snow from the mountains, the soil is highly fertile, yielding potatoes, cereal crops, vegetables and fruit. Traditionally the land was irrigated by canvas-sailed windmills – the familiar symbols of Lasíthiou – but these have gradually given way to the more efficient (if considerably less picturesque) diesel pumps. A few of the originals survive, and there is a row of ruined stone windmills at the Selí Ambélou Pass which heralds the plateau on its northern side. A circular road skirts the plateau (► 59), passing through small villages with their simple tavernas and craft shops. To avoid the tour crowds at the Díktaean Cave (► 49), arrive very early in the morning or leave it until the early evening.

The village of Kritsá, nestling on the hillside, makes a popular excursion from Agíos Nikólaos

🕂	29E2
✉	10km southwest of Ágios Nikólaos
🍴	Tavernas (£–£££)
🚌	Several a day from Ágios Nikólaos
♿	None
↔	Lató (► 54)
❓	Re-enactment of Cretan weddings in August

🕂	29E2
✉	Southwest of Ágios Nikólaos
🍴	Taverna Kronío, Tzermiádho (£)
🚌	Buses make a circular tour of the plateau, stopping at all villages
♿	No access possible to Díktaean Cave, but villages can be visited
↔	Díktaean Cave (► 49), Néapoli (► 56)

Old traditions die hard among the farming communities who work on the fields of the Lasíthiou Plateau

Dorian Lató; hill-top ruins with magnificent views down to the coast

LATÓ ✪✪

The remains of this Dorian town (7th–3rd century BC) occupy a magnificent site, spread on a saddle between two peaks above the Kritsá plain. Relatively few visitors come here, favouring instead the more ancient Minoan sites; but the views alone, encompassing sea and mountains, are worth the visit. The layout of Lató is somewhat simpler than that of the Minoan sites and the extensive ruins, rising in tiers, are notable for the massive stone blocks used in their construction including the entrance gateway, the guard towers, the deep workshops with their wells, the olive presses and the corn-grinding querns. A stepped street with houses and workshops leads up to the central *agora* – the meeting place and cult centre – with a shrine and a deep rainwater cistern. A broad stairway leads up to two council chambers, lined with benches and two archive rooms. A second stairway leads to a raised terrace with the remains of a temple and altar and a view of the ruined temple on the southeastern hill.

📍 29E2
✉ 3.5km north of Kritsá, 10km west of Ágios Nikólaos
🕐 Tue–Sun 8:30–3
🍴 Tavernas in Kritsá (£–££)
🚌 Buses from Kritsá
♿ None
💷 Free
↔ Panagía Kerá (➤ 26), Kritsá (➤ 53)

MAKRYGIALOS ✪✪

With one of the best beaches on Crete's southeast coast, the fishing village of Makrygialos and its sister village Análipsi is a small but growing resort. Hotel development along the main road hides its charms, but head dwon to the waterfront for a delightful view of its curving sandy beach lined with pleasant tavernas where fresh fish is always on the menu. The shallow water is warm and great for children.

📍 29E1
✉ 24km east of Ierápetra
🕐 Tue–Sun 8:30–3
🍴 Tavernas on the seafront (£–££)
🚌 Buse service from Ierápetra and Siteía
♿ None   ↔ Siteía (➤ 57)

MÓCHLOS ✪

From the main E75 between Ágios Nikólaos and Siteía, a minor road snakes down to the fishing village of Móchlos, a peaceful place, with seaside tavernas and a pebble beach. Excavations on the offshore island – once joined to the mainland – revealed the remains of what is believed to be a Minoan harbour town. Finds included ancient seal stones and tombs containing precious vases. A trip to the island can be made with one of the local fishermen (ask at one of the tavernas).

➕ 29E2
✉ 40km east of Ágios Nikólaos
🍴 Fish tavernas (£–££) on the seafront
🚌 None
♿ None

MONÍ TOPLOÚ ✪✪✪

Square and solid, the monastery of Toploú lies isolated in the barren hills east of Siteía. Built in the 14th century, it was fortified to resist pirate attacks and named after a large cannon (toploú in Turkish) which was used against invaders. Today it is one of the richest monasteries in Crete. Geared to tourism, the complex may have lost some of its charm as a working monastery, but it certainly merits a visit, particularly for the icons and delightful cobbled courtyard overlooked by three tiers of monks' cells. The most notable of the many icons in the church is the remarkably detailed *Lord Thou Art Great* (1770), by Ionnis Kornaros. Beyond the church are engravings, icons and a display about the role which the monastery played against the Turks during the Cretan struggle for independence and during World War II.

➕ 29F2
✉ 16km east of Siteía
☎ (28430) 61226
🕐 Daily 9–1, 2–6
🍴 Café/snack bar (£)
🚌 Bus service from Siteía then 3km walk from the main road
♿ Few
💷 Moderate
↔ Vái Beach (▶ 58)

The tranquil courtyard of the monastery of Toploú, with stairways leading up to the monks' cells

✚ 29E2
✉ 21km northwest of Ágios Nikólaos
🍴 Tavernas in the main square (£)
♿ None
🚌 Regular service from Irákleio and Ágios Nikólaos

✚ 29F2
✉ 18km east of Siteía
🍴 Elena (£)
🚌 Services from Siteía, Vái and Káto Zákros
ℹ Tourist office, Palaíkastro
☎ (28430) 61225
♿ Roussolakos free
♿ None
↔ Vái Beach (➤ 58)

Below: *the red rooftops of Neápoli*
Inset: *a taverna owner enjoys a glass of* soumádha

NEÁPOLI ★

A pleasant provincial town and former capital of Lasíthiou, Neápoli makes an obvious starting point for an excursion to the Lasíthiou Plateau (➤ 53). Few tourists visit the town, but if you are passing by it is worth stopping at one of the cafés or tavernas in the main square to sample the speciality of the town, *soumádha*, a sweet drink made of almonds. A small museum on the square houses crafts and a handful of local archaeological finds.

PALAÍKASTRO ★

Close to the coast and surrounded by olive groves, Palaíkastro makes a useful base for tourists wanting to explore the sandy beaches, archaeological sites and other attractions at the eastern end of the island. Expanding rapidly, the village has simple hotel accommodation, numerous rooms to rent, a handful of tavernas and bars and even its own tourist office. About 1.5km from the village, near the south end of Chiona beach, lie the partially excavated remains of Roussolakos, one of the largest Minoan towns discovered. Excavations are still in progress and the site – mainly of interest to specialists – is open to the public. Aretefacts from the site are displayed in the archaeological museums of Siteía and Irákleio. There are good sandy beaches to the south of Palaíkastro, and between the village and Vái to the north. On this stretch of the coast, Koureménos beach is a good place for windsurfing.

PANAGÍA KERÁ (➤ 26, TOP TEN)

Siteía's tightly packed houses overlook the harbour. Steep streets climb up the hill behind

SITEÍA ★★★

The most easterly town in Crete, at the end of the national highway, Siteía feels quite remote. Both a working port and tourist resort, it is a pleasant, leisurely place, particularly around the taverna-lined quayside and the older streets above the harbour. The town dates back to Graeco-Roman times, possibly even as far back as the Minoan era, but it was under the Venetians that the port had its heyday. Today it is essentially modern, with buildings set in tiers on the hillside. The only evidence of Venetian occupation is the fortress above the bay, reduced to a shell by the Turks, but used now as an open-air theatre. Siteía's long sandy beach, popular with windsurfers, stretches east from the town, followed by the parallel coastal road.

The **Archaiologikó Mouseío** (**Archaeological Museum**), just out of the centre, has a good collection of Minoan works of art, with useful explanations in English. Particularly interesting is the section devoted to Zákros Palace (➤ 58), with decorated vessels, urns, cooking pots, a wine press and a collection of clay tablets with the rare Linear A script (➤ 78). In the entrance hall pride of place goes to the ivory statuette of a young man (c1450) discovered at Palaíkaistro. The small **Folk Museum**, up from the harbour, has a collection of finely made traditional crafts, including baskets for carrying grapes, and bedspreads and rugs coloured with dye from indigenous plants.

✠ 29F2
✉ 70km east of Ágios Nikólaos
🍴 Kastro (££)
🚌 Services from Ágios Nikólaos, Irákleio and Ierápetra

Archaeological Museum
✉ Odós Piskokéfalou 3
☎ (28430) 23917
🕐 Tue–Sun 8:30–3
♿ Few
💰 Moderate; free on Sun in winter

Folk Museum
✉ Odós Kapetán Sifi 28
☎ (28430) 22861
🕐 May–Oct Mon–Sat 9:30–3 (also Wed 5–8)
♿ Ground floor only
💰 Inexpensive

Did you know ?

Siteía is one of the best wine-producing regions in Crete. Both its red and white wines are delicious. You can tase them at the wine co-operative, on the main road into town, which gives free tours in summer. Siteía is also known for its olive oil and sultanas, and a Sultana Festival takes place here in August.

VÁI BEACH ✪✪✪

Backed by a plantation of rare date palms, the tropical-looking Vái beach lies at the northeastern tip of the island. The remote location is no deterrent and the lovely sandy bay is invariably crowded in summer. To see it at its best you must come early in the morning or off-season. Formerly frequented by backpackers, who stayed overnight on the sands, the beach is now strictly regulated, with a camping ban, car park charges and an extensive range of beach facilities.

➕ 29F2
✉ 9km north of Palaíkastro
🍴 Taverna (££) on the beach
🚌 Service to Palaíkastro and Siteía
♿ Good
🅿 Car park charges

Below: *Vái beach*
Bottom: *Zakros Palace*

ZÁKROS PALACE ✪✪✪

Part of the appeal of the Minoan palace of Zákros is the remote valley setting by the coast, seemingly far removed from civilisation. However, in Minoan times this was a major centre, linked to a port (now submerged), trading with Egypt and the Middle East. It wasn't until the 1960s that a Greek professor, Nikólaos Pláton, discovered the palace and its archaeological treasures, their quantity and quality suggesting a highly affluent community.

For an overall view of the setting and layout, start at the upper town; then climb down to the lower level and central court. From here, explore the ceremonial hall, a small banqueting hall and a cluster of other rooms, then cross to the royal apartments. The south side of the central court is bordered by workshops, and in the southeast corner excavators discovered 3,500-year-old olives preserved in water at the bottom of a jar. Treasures from the palace are housed in the Archaeological Museum at Irákleio (➤ 17, 18) and Siteía's museum (➤ 57).

➕ 29F2
✉ Káto Zákros
☎ (28430) 26897
🕐 Daily Apr–Oct 8–5; Nov–Mar Tue–Sun 8–3
🍴 Maria, Káto Zákros (£)
🚌 Twice a day in summer
♿ None
🅿 Moderate; free on Sun in winter

Around the Lasíthiou Plateau

The tour starts from Neápoli but can also be approached from Ágios Nikólaos or the north coast. Take non-slip shoes and a torch for the caves.

Follow the sign for Lasíthiou from the main square in Neápoli. The road twists its way scenically up through the mountains.

Stop at the café at Zénia for a break from the bends and a breathtaking view of the Díktaean peaks.

Continue up through villages where locals sell wine, rakí and honey by the roadside.

After about 27km, the plateau comes suddenly and spectacularly into view. Stop by the roadside to look down on to the flat plain, encircled by soaring mountains.

After the village of Mesa Lasíthiou, turn right at the road junction for Tzermiádho (signposted to Dzermido).

Signed from the main road, the Krónio Cave (also known as the Cave of Trápeza) was used as a burial site from prehistoric times. Around 1km from the parking area, there are (optional) guides to show you the way.

Continue along the road encircling the plateau. At the junction at Pinakianó go straight on, following signs for Psychró. Beyond the village of Pláti, follow signs for the Díktaean Cave.

This is Crete's most famous cave (▶ 49), the so-called birthplace of Zeus.

Continue around the plateau until you reach the village of Ágios Geórgios which has a folk museum, well signed from the centre.

At Ágios Konstantínos the full circle of the plateau has been completed. Turn right to return to Neápoli.

Distance
83km

Time
6–7 hours, including stops and lunch

Start/End Point
Neápoli
✚ 29E2

Lunch
Taverna Kronio (£)
✉ Tzermiádho
☎ (28440) 22375

The road winds its way up through rugged mountains to reach the spectacular Lasíthiou Plateau

In the Know

If you only have a short time to visit Crete, or would like to get a real flavour of the country, here are some ideas:

10
Ways to Be a Local

Always refer to the locals as Cretans, rather than Greeks.

Eat late (lunch around 2PM, dinner 9PM), otherwise you'll miss the action.

Allow a good hour or more for lunch or dinner. Greek meals are for lingering and the service is rarely fast.

Take a siesta to avoid the afternoon sun. Avoid making telephone calls between 3PM–5PM when most of the locals are resting.

Try out the local *kafenion* (traditional café). Ask for Greek coffee (*ellenikós kafés*) – never for Turkish coffee, which may offend.

Join the *voltá*, the early evening stroll; or sit at a café and watch the world go by.

Mingle with the locals in the morning markets and buy fruit, cheese and spices.

Readily accept Cretan hospitality. You are not expected to return it and refusing it may offend.

Join the locals in Greek traditional dancing at a taverna.

Show due respect in churches, chapels and monasteries by dressing modestly.

10
Good Places to Have Lunch

Akrogiali (£££) It is well worth a taxi ride from Chaniá for this outstanding fish restaurant at the town beach. ✉ Akti Papanikoli 20, Nea Hora, Chaniá ☎ (28210) 71110 🕐 Mon–Sat 7PM–midnight

Ippokambos (£) This is one of the liveliest places in town, so get there early or expect to wait. The excellent-value fish dishes and large choice of *mezédes* in this simple taverna near Irákleio's harbour makes it popular with locals. ✉ Sófokli Venizélou, Irákleio ☎ (28210) 280240 🕐 Daily

I Tráta (££) Close to the small town beach of Kitroplatía, the taverna has an inviting rooftop terrace and a menu offering a variety of fish, grilled meat and local Greek fare. ✉ Akti Pagkalou 17 ☎ (28410) 22028 🕐 Daily 11AM–midnight

Karnagio (££) Set just back from the waterfront on the square by the old Customs House, this draws tourists and Cretans alike for its Cretan specialities and friendly atmosphere. ✉ 8 Plateía Katehákí, Old Port, Chaniá ☎ (28410) 53366 🕐 Apr–Oct daily 8AM–2AM

Kastro (££) This comfortable taverna has a splendid location with outdoor tables on the harbourside. Fresh fish and seafood are available most days, and the moussaka is particularly tasty. ✉ Odós Venizélou 169, Siteía ☎ (28430) 23649 🕐 Daily 9AM–1AM

Limani (££) With shaded outdoor tables right beside the beach, this popular fish taverna makes a good mid-day break. The Cretan specialities are also excellent.. ✉ On the Makrygialos waterfront ☎ (28430) 52457 🕐 Daily 10AM–noon

Mythos (£–££) The breezy seaside terrace makes this

Above: *the covered market in Chaniá*. Right: *a Cretan farmer*

Joining the dancing at a taverna

traditional taverna well worth a stop on a hot day. Good value, and there are several daily specials.
✉ Kalives, 20km east of Chaniá ☎ (28250) 31964 🕐 Daily noon–late

Seven Brothers (££) One of several restaurants on Réthymno's inner harbour, serving fresh charcoal-grilled fish, lobster and meat. ✉ Réthymno Harbour ☎ (0831) 28956 🕐 All day, every day

Taverna Votomos (££) Fresh trout from the nearby hatchery is the speciality at this taverna next to the Idi Hotel, with a pleasant rural setting beside a small stream. ✉ Zaros, just outside town ☎ (28940) 31302 🕐 Daily 11AM– midnight, weekends only in winter

Vritomartes (££) Fresh seafood tops the menu at this popular taverna and you can't beat the location; right in the centre of the harbour. ✉ Sfiraki waterfront Eloúnta ☎ (28410) 41325 🕐 Apr-Oct, daily 10AM–11PM

10
Top Activities

Walking through the spectacular Samariá Gorge (➤ 20, 83) or one of the shorter, equally scenic gorges in the Chaniá region.

Exploring ancient Minoan palaces (Knosós, Mália, Faistós and Zákros).

Taking a boat trip or ferry to one of the offshore islands or unspoilt coastal villages.

Swimming from one of Crete's many inviting sandy beaches.

Savouring the bustling atmosphere of the old streets of Chaniá, Irákleio and Réthymno.

Learning to scuba dive in the crystal clear waters.

Hiking in the Levká Óri or in one of the other mountain ranges.

Hiring a car to escape the tourist haunts and explore the peaceful countryside.

Cycling down a mountain – after being driven to the top.

Relaxing in a beach taverna, watching the sunset and savouring simple Greek food.

10
Best Beaches

Elafonísi Idyllic pink-tinged sands, in a semi-tropical lagoon. (➤ 80)

Falásarna Huge, beautiful sandy beach, with remarkably few tourists. (➤ 81)

Frangkokástelo Fine sands and clear waters, suitable for snorkelling. (➤ 82)

Georgioúpoli Fine sandy beach stretching several kilometres to the east. (➤ 86)

Mátala Beautiful but often crowded south-coast bay, famous for its rock caves. (➤ 41)

Préveli Idyllic creek with a grove of date palms. (➤ 70)

Stavrós Scenic bay and beach, with clear shallow waters, on Akrotíri peninsula. (➤ 92)

Sweetwater Beach Long pebble beach known for freshwater springs and nudist campers, reached

---

by boat or foot from Loutró or Chóra Sfakíon. (➤ 80)

Vái Semi-tropical, otherwise known as Palm Beach. Arrive early to avoid the crowds. (➤ 58)

Yaidhouronísi Uninhabited island with exotic beaches, reached by excursion boat. (➤ 84)

10
Best Drinks and Food

Rakí The ubiquitous local firewater, made from the skins and seeds of grapes.

Oúzo A Greek aniseed-flavour aperitif, like Pernod.

Mournoraki A brandy made from mulberries, from the Réthymno area.

Mandarini A locally produced tangerine liqueur.

Fresh orange juice squeezed from juicy local oranges, the most refreshing soft drink in Crete.

Tirópitta Warm pastries filled with feta cheese. Spinach pies (*spanakópita*) are also good.

Giaoúrti kai méli Sheep's milk yoghurt with thyme-flavoured honey.

Fruit Cherries, melons, grapes, oranges, apricots, plums and figs are grown here.

Mezédes Savoury snacks such as fried squid, octopus, feta cheese, snails and olives.

Cretan Cheese Apart from feta, try *graviéra* or *myzíthra*.

Réthymno Province

Réthymno is the smallest and most mountainous of Crete's four provinces. To the east it is bordered by the towering peaks of the Psiloreítis range, to the west by the Levká Ori or White Mountains. Between the two lies the beautiful green Amári Valley, where mountain hamlets seem lost in time. On the north coast the main attraction is the delightful historic town of Réthymno. Sandy beaches stretch either side of the provincial capital, and the coast to the east is built up with a long ribbon of tourist development. South coast development is restricted by the wild coastline of cliffs and headlands, and some bays are accessible only on foot or by dirt track. Agía Galíni and Plakiás are – for the moment – the only two resorts developed for package holidays. The main cultural attractions are the famous monasteries of Arkádi and Préveli.

> *'I was with Hercules and Cadmus once, when in a wood of Crete they bay'd the bear with hounds of Sparta: never did I hear... so musical a discord, such sweet thunder.'*

WILLIAM SHAKESPEARE
Hippolyta in *A Midsummer Night's Dream* (c1596)

———————●———————

Left: *the Amári valley.* Above: *Réthymno's Venetian fortifications*

63

The Porta Guora in Réthymno is the only surviving remnant of the Venetian city walls

The minaret soaring above the town was built during the 250-year period of Turkish rule

Réthymno Town

Réthymno was a town of little significance until the 16th and 17th centuries when it prospered under the Venetians. Following the fall of Constantinople, many Byzantine scholars sought refuge here and the town became an important intellectual and cultural centre. In 1646 it came under Turkish rule, which lasted 250 years. The old quarter retains much of its Venetian and Turkish character and the town is still regarded as the 'intellectual capital' of the island.

The dominant feature of the town is the mighty Venetian fortress, built to defend the city against pirate attacks. To the east lies the harbour, where the waterside fish tavernas are a magnet for tourists. The narrow, pedestrianised alleys of the old town are ideal for strolling. Down virtually every street there are fascinating architectural details to admire, such as ornately carved Venetian doorways and arches, the Turkish overhanging wooden balconies and the minarets and domes which lend an exotic air to the skyline. Tiny shops are crammed with *objets d'art*, craftsmen sell leather or jewellery, grocery stores are stocked with herbs, spices and *rakí*. At the end of a morning's stroll head for the Rimondi Fountain, select from one of the surrounding *al fresco* cafés and tavernas and watch the world go by.

The town has a wide sandy beach, backed by a palm-lined promenade and tavernas, hotels and cafés. The sands are packed in summer, but there are quieter beaches with cleaner waters away to the east and west.

A Walk Around Réthymno

The walk starts at the Venetian Harbour.

Make for the fortress, which is located to the west, taking the narrow Odós Makedónias beyond the Hotel Ideon. Opposite the entrance of the fort, the Archaeological Museum (➤ 66) is well worth a visit.

Wander among the ruins within the ramparts (➤ 66) and admire the views.

Just below the museum take the street to the centre which is signed Kanakakis Gallery, and, at the end of the street, turn left and then right for the street which brings you to Fountain Square.

Erected by the Venetians, the splendid Rimondi Fountain (1623) has four Corinthian columns flanking water-spouting lions' heads.

Turn right down Odós Arambatzoglou, left at the square at the end and immediately left again. Along this narrow street you will find the Folk Museum (➤ 67) and the Nerantziés Mosque (➤ 67).

At the end of the street, turn right into the busy Ethníkos Antistáseos, with a wide variety of shops and a market at the far end. Beyond the 16th-century city gate you can see the public gardens, venue of the July Wine Festival.

Retrace your steps along Ethníkos Antistáseos.

Plateía Petiháki, the hub of the old town, is lined with tavernas and cafés.

Turn right at the end by the fountain to walk along Odós Paleológou.

The elegant Loggia at the end of the street was the meeting place of Venetian nobility. Today it is the museum shop for the Ministry of Culture.

Distance
Just over 2km

Time
2–3 hours including sightseeing

Start point
Harbour
✚ 28C2

End point
Loggia
✚ 28C2

Lunch
Kypia Maria (£)
✉ Odós Moshovitou 20
☎ (28310) 29078

A cobbled alley leads to the Venetian Walls which incorporate a mosque and the ruins of magazines and barracks

What to See in Réthymno

➕ 28C2
✉ Fortétza
☎ (28310) 54668
🕐 Tue–Sun 8:30–3
🍴 Centre of town (£–£££)
♿ None
💵 Moderate
↔ Centre of Contemporary
Art (see below)

ARCHAIOLOGIKÓ MOUSEÍO ✪✪
(ARCHAEOLOGICAL MUSEUM)

Occupying the former Turkish prison at the entrance to the fortress, this is now a modern, well-organised museum of Minoan and Graeco-Roman finds from the Réthymno region. Especially noteworthy are the grave goods and decorated sarcophagi from the late Minoan period, some of them embellished with hunting scenes.

➕ 28C2
✉ Odós Chimárras
☎ (28310) 52530
🕐 Apr–Oct Tue–Fri 9–1,
7–10, Sat and Sun 11–3;
Nov–Mar Tue–Sun 10–2,
6–9
🍴 In old town (£–£££)
♿ None
💵 Moderate

CENTRE OF CONTEMPORARY ART ✪

This modern art centre is also known as the L Kanakakis Gallery. The stylish whitewashed galleries on two floors host temporary exhibitions of modern painting, sculpture and other media, mainly by Greek artists. It also has a collection of Greek art (only part of which is on view at any one time), including 70 paintings by Lefteris Kanakakis, a local artist.

Right: *Réthymno's
imposing Venetian
fortress provides
panoramic views over the
town, coast and
countryside*
Below: *monks are not an
unusual sight, even in
modern Crete*

FORTÉTZA (VENETIAN FORTRESS) ✪✪✪

At the far end of the promontory, above the town, the Venetian fortress was built in 1573–1586 to stem the fearsome Turkish attacks on the city. Believed to be the largest Venetian fort ever built, it was designed to protect the entire population of the town. When the Turks attacked in 1646, the Venetian troops took cover here, along with several thousand townspeople; but following a siege of just 23 days, the fortress surrendered. Today the outer walls are well preserved, but most of the buildings were destroyed by earthquakes or by bombs in World War II. Inside the walls the dominant feature is a mosque built for the Turkish garrison and recently restored. Only ruins survive from the garrison quarters, the governor's residence, powder magazines and other buildings, but the atmosphere is very evocative and there are fine views of the town and coast. Plays and concerts take place here during the summer months.

🌐 28C2
✉ Odós Katecháki
☎ (28310) 28101
🕐 Tue–Sun 9–6; longer hours in summer
🍴 Café (£)
♿ None
💷 Moderate
🔁 Archaeological Museum, Centre of Contemporary Art (➤ 66)

Did you know ?

Réthymno's small harbour, built originally by the Venetians in the 13th century, has a history of silting up. It is continually being dredged and the only boat of any size that docks here is the Piraeus (Athens) ferry. The inner harbour is just used for fishing boats and pleasure craft – a picturesque scene which pushes up the prices in the harbourside tavernas.

MOUSEÍO ISTORIAS KAI LAÍKIS TÉCHNIS (HISTORICAL AND FOLK MUSEUM) ✪✪

The museum moved in 1995 from its previous site in Mesolongiou to the more spacious setting of a finely restored Venetian house, with a garden, near the Nerantziés Mosque. The galleries house a charming collection of crafts from local homes, including fine samples of embroidery, lace, basketware, pottery, knives and agricultural tools. Explanations, translated into English, accompany displays of bread-making techniques, Greek needlework and other traditional rural crafts.

🌐 28C2
✉ Odós Vernardóu
☎ (28310) 23398
🕐 Mon–Sat 9:30–2; Wed, Fri 9–2 in winter
🍴 Cafés and tavernas in Plateía Petiháki (£–££)
♿ Few
💷 Moderate
🔁 Nerantziés Mosque (see below)

TEMENOS NERANTZE (NERANTZIÉS MOSQUE) ✪

South of the Rimondi Fountain, the three-domed mosque's finest feature is its soaring minaret. Originally the Church of Santa Maria, it was converted into a mosque by the Turks shortly after their defeat of Réthymno. The minaret was added in 1890 and, prior to closure for safety reasons, afforded splendid views of the town. Today the mosque is a music school and concert hall.

🌐 28C2
✉ Odós Vernadóu 28–30
☎ (28310) 23398;
🕐 Closed to public except for concerts
🍴 Cafés and tavernas in Plateía Petiháki (£–££)
🔁 Folk Museum (see above)

Pottery on Crete is good value

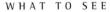

What to See in Réthymno Province

AGÍA GALÍNI ⭐

At the foot of the Amári valley, with houses, hotels and apartments stacked up on the hillside, Agía Galíni has grown from a remote fishing village into a fully-fledged tourist resort. The lively, narrow streets of the centre lead down to a harbour of fishing boats and pleasure cruisers and are packed with tavernas, bars and souvenir shops. It is a friendly, cheerful place, but it can become claustrophobic in high season and there is an alarming amount of further construction on the way. The resort beach of stony, dark grey sand to the east of the village is not ideal but there are boats to the more attractive beaches of Ágios Geórgios and Ágios Pávlos to the west, and daily cruises to the lovely sandy beaches of the Paximádia Islands, 12km off shore.

28C1
54km southeast of Réthymno
Onar (££)
Services to Irákleio, Réthymno, Faistós and Mátala
Not very suitable – narrow steep streets
Faistós (➤ 19), Agía Triáda (➤ 16), Museum of Cretan Ethnology at Voroí (➤ 43)

ANÓGIA ⭐⭐

Lying below the peaks of the Psiloreítis range, Anógia is the last village before the Ídaean Cave, and the main starting point for the hike up to the summit (see Mount Psiloreítis, ➤ 69). The village is best known for its crafts, particularly handwoven blankets, rugs, wall hangings and embroidery, all of which you will see on display in the shops. Women at their looms give the village the air of a long-established settlement, but while old traditions survive, all the buildings are new. During World War II, General Kreipe, Commander-in-Chief of the German forces, was kidnapped by partisans and hidden in Anógia, before being removed from Crete. In retaliation the Germans destroyed the entire village, apart from the church, and killed many of the menfolk.

28C2
35km west of Irákleio
A couple of simple tavernas (£) in the village
Service from Irákleio and Réthymno
Steep roads, not very suitable

Spinning in the mountain village of Anógia – an old way of life caters to tourist demands

BALÍ ✪

On the north coast, east of Réthymno, Balí is a small but growing resort of rocky coves and tiny sand and shingle beaches. The one-time fishing village is now built up with hotels and apartments, and life here centres primarily on tavernas, bars and discos. Paradise Beach (also known as Evita Beach) is the best place to swim, but the beach is incredibly crowded in summer. Apart from watersports and boat trips to Réthymno there is not a great deal to do here, but Balí is situated roughly half-way between Irákleio and Réthymno, and only 2km from the national highway, so there are plenty of opportunities for excursions.

MONÍ ARKÁDIOU (► 24, TOP TEN)

OROS PSILOREÍTIS ✪✪✪
(MOUNT PSILOREÍTIS)

At 2,456m, Mount Psiloreítis, or Mount Ída, is the highest point on Crete. From Anógia (► 68) a winding road through barren, mountainous terrain leads to the Nída Plateau at the foot of the mountain. Near the end of the road, by the taverna, a path leads up to the Idaiki Spiliá (Ídaean Cave), a contender, along with the Diktaean Cave (► 49), for the title of birthplace of Zeus. Excavations in the 1880s yielded bronze shields from the 9th and 8th centuries BC, suggesting that the cave was a post-Minoan cult centre. You can walk down into the cave, but it is fairly shallow with no dramatic natural rock formations. The path to the summit of Mount Psiloreítis also starts at the taverna – a gruelling 7–8 hour return trip.

🞖 28C2
✉ 30km east of Réthymno
🍴 Harbourside tavernas (£–££)
🚌 2km from bus stop for service to Irákleio and Réthymno
♿ Steep streets, not suitable
🔄 Melidóni Cave (► 70)

*Above: local crafts are sold from stalls in Anógia
Below: bags are popular*

🞖 28C2
✉ 17km south of Anógia to base of mountain
🍴 None
♿ Not suitable
🔄 Anógia (► 68)

PLAKIÁS ✪

A rapidly expanding resort, Plakiás' main asset is its setting, with a long sweep of beach surrounded by steep mountains. It is a fairly low-key place with hotels and apartments, a couple of discos and several beach tavernas with lovely views of the sunset. The beach of shingle and coarse sand is rather exposed, but there's a better one at Damnóni, reached by car or a 30-minute walk.

28C2
22km southwest of Spíli
Beach tavernas (£–££)
Regular service to Réthymno
Moní Préveli (➤ 25), Préveli Beach (below)
Few

PRÉVELI BEACH ✪✪

The beautiful sandy cove at the mouth of the Kourtalióti Gorge can be reached by boat or by a steep and demanding walk from Moní Préveli (➤ 25). It is also known as Palm Beach, after the date palms that line the banks of the River Megapótomos, which flows into the sea at Préveli. Idyllic off-season, the beach fills to overflowing with boatloads of tourists in the summer.

28C2
38km south of Réthymno
Two tavernas (£)
Day trips from Plakiás and Agía Galini
None
Moní Préveli (➤ 25)

SPÍLAIO TOU MEDLIDÓNI (MELIDÓNI CAVE) ✪✪

Mythical home of Talos, the bronze giant who guarded the coasts of Crete, the Melidóni Cave has some splendid stalactites and stalagmites. But it is not so much the natural beauty of the cave as its tragic history that has earned it fame. In 1824 around 370 of the villagers, mostly women, children and the elderly, hid here from the Turks. Turkish troops laid siege to the cave but the villagers refused to surrender and shot two of the enemy. In retaliation the Turks blocked the entrance of the caves, trying to suffocate the Cretans. Then they lit fires at the cave mouth, asphyxiating everyone inside. An ossiary in one of the chambers still contains the victims' bones, and an annual commemoration service is held in the local church.

28C2
4km northeast of Pérama, a short drive or 30 minutes' walk from the village of Melidóni.
(28340) 22046
Apr–Nov daily 9–6:30/7
Bar by the cave (£)
Moderate
Balí (➤ 69)

Préveli beach, where a palm-fringed estuary meets the sea

Amári Valley Drive

Dwarfed on the east side by the Psiloreítis massif, the fertile Amári valley offers glorious views.

From Réthymno head east on the old national highway, turning right at the sign for Amári. At the village of Agía Fotinís go straight on, then turn left for Thrónos.

Thrónos has a lovely church with medieval frescoes and an early Byzantine mosaic pavement. (Ask locally for the key if the church is locked.) Beyond the church a path leads up to the ruins of the ancient city of Sybrito.

Return to the main road and continue to Moní Asomáton where Venetian monastery buildings are occupied by an agricultural college. After another 2km turn right for Amári (5km).

Amári has wonderful valley views and some faded frescoes in the Church of Agía Ánna.

Returning to the main road, turn right for Vizári which has Roman and Byzantine remains. After Nithavris (11km) take the road east to Zarós (24km).

An attractive mountain village, Zarós is famous for its springs. Stop for lunch at one of the tavernas serving trout.

Return towards Réthymno, this time taking the road on the west side of the valley, to reach Gerakári.

Gerakári is famous for its cherry trees, and you can buy bottled cherries and cherry brandy in the village. At Méronas, 4km beyond Gerakári, admire the views across the valley and the frescoes in Panagía church.

Back at Agía Fotínís, turn left to return to Réthymno.

Distance
165km

Time
With stops and lunch allow a full day

Start/End Point
Réthymno
✚ 28C2

Lunch
Taverna Votomos (££)
✉ Zarós
☎ (28940) 31302

Above: *Thrónos, in the Amári valley, has a beautifully frescoed 14th- century church*

Below: *a farming family, though many young people now work in tourism*

Food & Drink

Food in Crete may not rank in the league of gourmet cuisine, but for many visitors there is nothing more pleasurable than whiling away the hours at a seaside taverna, savouring a simple home-cooked meal and a glass or two of Cretan wine.

Greek Food

Establishments serving the traditional Cretan home cooking are well worth seeking out – no-frills tavernas, patronised by locals, that are usually found in back streets or rural areas, well away from tourist centres.

Greek menus normally offer a wide choice of starters, followed by meat, fish or vegetable dishes. Frequently, diners are invited into the kitchen to lift the lids and see what's cooking. Typical starters (*mezédes*), served with a basket of bread, are *taramósalata* (smoked and puréed cod's roe), *tzatsíki* (yoghurt, cucumber and garlic), filo pastry pies, *dolmádhes* (stuffed vine leaves with rice), *khoriatíki* (Greek salad with tomatoes, cucumber, olives and feta cheese) and *melitzanosaláta* (puréed aubergine). Fresh seafood, such as red mullet, swordfish, sea bream, prawns and lobster, is increasingly hard to come by and is invariably expensive, particularly at harbourside restaurants. Cheaper choices are octopus, squid, whitebait or sardines. In a restaurant the catch of the day will vary according to the time of the year and will normally just be marked 'fresh fish' on the menu with a price per kilo. It's perfectly acceptable to ask the waiter if you can see the fish, and find out what the actual price will be. Seafood such as large succulent prawns, squid, octopus and cuttle fish are likely to be frozen. Although tavernas are obliged to specify on the menu which fish is frozen, many of them don't bother.

The most commonplace meat dish is *souvlaki*, small cubes of pork (or occasionally other types of meat or fish), roasted on a skewer and served with bread, chips and salad. Most menus also feature *moussaká* (minced meat with aubergines and cheese), *stifado* (a meat or fish casserole baked with herbs and tomatoes), and *pastitsio* (macaroni baked with meat). Lamb and chicken, either grilled, roasted or cooked in a casserole, are available in the majority of tavernas. Vegetables are locally grown and particularly delicious. Tomatoes, peppers, aubergines or

Every menu features a Greek salad – a colourful combination of feta cheese, tomatoes, cucumber, onion and herbs

other seasonal vegetables are cooked in olive oil, or often served stuffed with minced meat, rice and herbs.

For a change from Greek fare (and menus tend to be similar wherever you go), there are plenty of places serving international dishes, particularly pasta and pizza; there are also a few Chinese restaurants in the main towns.

Desserts and Pastries

For dessert locals tend to go to the local pastry shop (*zakharoplasteío*), which will have a choice of *baklavá* (filo pastry with honey and nuts), *kataifa* (shredded pastry with walnuts and syrup) and other sticky treats. Other calorific favourites are *loukoumádes* (small round, deep-fried fritters in syrup, served warm), and *bougátsa*, a creamy custard pastry dusted with icing sugar. Cheese pastries (➤ 61) make delicious snacks and are often served with honey as a dessert.

Drinking

All restaurants serve Cretan wines, some also have a choice of other Greek varieties and a handful among the more formal restaurants have an international wine list. The dry Cretan bottled red and white wines go well with the oily food; the cheap house wine from the barrel, served in tin jugs, traditionally by the kilo, is often surprisingly good. After a meal you may well be offered a complimentary thimble full of *rakí* (➤ 61), perhaps accompanied by a tiny portion of *baklavá* or other sweet.

All bars serve beer – locally-brewed Mythos, Amstel and Henninger or imported Heineken and Lowenbrau.

Locally grown vegetables, stuffed with meat and rice, make a wholesome and reasonably priced meal

No holiday in Greece is complete without a taste of the spirit, ouzo, or the local rakí

Chaniá Province

The most westerly province in Crete, Chaniá has no great archaeological sites but it provides some of the most spectacular scenery on the island. Views are dominated by the majestic peaks of the Levká Óri (White Mountains), snow-capped for six months of the year. On the south coast the mountains drop abruptly to the Libyan Sea, leaving little space for any major development. Compared to the flatter north coast, the south is sparsely populated, with just a handful of villages nestling below the mountains and a couple of holiday resorts with beaches. Spectacular, walkable gorges are a feature of the White Mountains, particularly the Samariá Gorge, which is the second most popular attraction in Crete. On the north coast the historic town of Chaniá, which incorporates the island's most beautiful harbour, makes a delightful base.

> *' Crete is a land amid the*
> *wine-dark sea,*
> *Fair and rich and sea-girt;*
> *it is well peopled,*
> *With great numbers living*
> *in ninety cities,*
> *Each speaking a different*
> *language. '*
> HOMER
> *The Odyssey (c700 BC)*

Left: *the picturesque harbourfront in Chaniá.* Above: *old doorway in Chaniá*

The elegant Venetian
lighthouse at Chaniá,
seen across the harbour
from Fort Firkás

Chaniá

The ancient city of Kydonía, inhabited since
neolithic times, became the most important centre
in Crete after the destruction of Knosós. The town
fell into decline under the Arabs, but during the
Venetian occupation (1290–1646) La Canea, as it
was renamed, became 'the Venice of the East'.
Following the Turkish occupation, which lasted
from 1646–1898, Chaniá was made capital of Crete
and remained so until 1971.

Chaniá is not only the best base for exploring
western Crete, it is arguably the island's most
appealing town. Beautifully set below the White
Mountains, it has a lively harbour, a maze of alleys
and a string of beaches nearby. Strolling is the
most pleasurable activity, either along the
harbourfront, or through the streets of the old
town, where Venetian and Turkish houses have
been elegantly restored. Along the narrow alleys
are such charming features as old portals and
overhanging balconies, as well as enticing hole-in-
the-wall craft shops and cafés.

The real magnet is the outer harbour, with its
faded, shuttered houses, and its crescent of cafés
and tavernas overlooking the water. This is where
the locals come for their early evening *vólta*. The inner
harbour, overlooked by Venetian arsenals, is another focal
point, with fishing boats, pleasure craft and tavernas.
Chaniá may be picturesque, but there are often too many
tourists crowding the narrow streets. To appreciate its
beauty, visit early or later in the day.

Chaniá's waterfront

What to See in Chaniá

ARCHAIOLOGIKÓ MOUSEÍO (ARCHAEOLOGICAL MUSEUM) ⭐⭐

The Church of St Francis was the largest church to be built in Chaniá during the Venetian era, and its spacious vaulted interior makes a handsome setting for the archaeological discoveries from excavations in the region. The exhibits span the period from late neolithic to Roman occupation, and greatly assist in adding a human dimension to the ancient sites of the area.

The majority of artefacts date from the late Minoan era and include pottery, weapons, seals, decorated clay tombs (*larnakes*) and tablets inscribed with Linéar A and B scripts (▶ 78).

The Graeco-Roman section is represented by a collection of sculpture and glassware, leading up to three fine Roman mosaics, which were discovered in villas in Chaniá, displayed at the far end of the church.

The little garden beside the church features a damaged Lion of St Mark, and a beautifully preserved ten-sided Turkish fountain, dating from the period when the church was converted by the Turks into a base of a minaret.

✚ 28B2
✉ Odós Khalídon, 21
☎ (28210) 90334
🕐 Tue–Sun 8:30–5; off-season Tue–Sun 8:30–3
🍴 Cafés and tavernas in Odós Khalídon or on the harbour (£–£££)
♿ Accessible to wheelchairs
👛 Moderate; free on Sun in winter

BYZANTINE MUSEUM ⭐

Chaniá's newest museum is housed in a small, renovated church on the western side of the fortress. Its displays incorporate a range of Byzantine artefacts, including mosaics, sculptures and jewellery as well as the usual collection of icons. A highlight is the icon of St George slaying the dragon, at the far end of the musem. It was painted by Emmanuel Tzanes Bouniales (1610–90), one of the foremost arists of the Cretan school of icon painters. Particularly oustanding too are the brightly coloured fragments of 11th-century wall frescoes. The San Salvatore collection, in a brightly lit side gallery, includes a beautiful display of glass bead necklaces, jewellery, crosses, ceramics, Byzantine coins and a rare bronze lamp from the 6th and 7th centuries. There are also some fascinating post-Byzantine artefacts, such as the curious horned mask from 16th–17th century Chaniá town. An excellent museum recalling Crete's past.

✚ 28B2
✉ Odós Theotokopoulou, 82
☎ (28210) 96046
🕐 Apr–Sep daily 8:30–5; Oct–Mar Tue–Sun 8:30–3
🍴 Cafés and tavernas in on the harbour (£–£££)
♿ Accessible
👛 Moderate; free on Sun in winter

Local woman in Chaniá

MOUSEÍO NAUTIKO (NAVAL MUSEUM) ✪✪

✚ 28B2
✉ Fort Firkas, Aktí Kountourioti
☎ (28210) 26437
🕐 Daily 9–4; 10–2 in winter
🍴 Harbour restaurants (£–£££)
♿ None
🎫 Moderate

Tracing Crete's sea trade and maritime warfare, the Naval Museum is housed in the restored Venetian Fírkas Tower guarding Chaniá's harbour. Most of the exhibits here are models of ships, ranging from the simple craft of the Copper Period (2800 BC) to submarines built in the 1980s. The collection also contains marine weapons and instruments, historical documents, a model of the Venetian town of La Canea and, on the first floor, an exhibition devoted to the World War II Battle of Crete in 1941. Beyond the gate, the strategically sited bastion commands impressive views of the harbour, the Venetian lighthouse and the domed Mosque of the Janissaries (built in 1645, following the Turkish conquest). It was here, at the Fírkas fortifications, that the Greek flag was first raised on Crete in November 1913.

Did you know ?

Sir Arthur Evans distinguished three phases in the Minoan script: hieroglyphics (c2000–1650 BC), Linear A (c1750–1450 BC) and Linear B (dates unknown but probably from 1450 or 1400 BC). Despite lengthy research, the first two have yet to be deciphered. Linear B, a form of Greek used by the Mycenaeans, was deciphered in the 1950s. The script has revealed fascinating details of the religion and economic history of the late Minoan civilisation.

A Walk Around Chaniá

Start at the Naval Museum (➤ 78), which is situated on the west side of the Old Harbour.

With the water on your right, walk along the exterior of the fortifications and cut inland along Odós Theotokopoúlou, a picturesque street with old Venetian houses and craft shops. At the end, turn left down Odós Zambelioú and at the main square turn right.

Odós Khalídon, lined with shops, is the tourist hub of Chaniá. On the right is the Archaeological Museum (➤ 77) and just beyond it, in the courtyard of the Catholic church, the small Folk Museum. On the other side of the road lie the Turkish Baths and a large square, overlooked by Chaniá's unremarkable cathedral.

Take the second left for Odós Skridlóf, a narrow alley packed with leather stalls, and go straight on for the covered market (➤ 106). Continuing along the same road, take the second street on the left for the delightful 16th-century Agíos Anárgyroi, housing ancient icons.

At end of the street the tree-lined Plateia 1821 is overlooked by Ágios Nikólaos, a former mosque which retains its soaring minaret.

At the opposite side of the square turn right for the Inner Harbour. Divert left along Odós Karnewáro to see the Greek/Swedish excavations which have revealed Minoan remains.

At the waterfront, on the right, are the vaults of the 16th century Venetian Arsenal. Fish tavernas overlook the colourful Inner Harbour. From here you can walk along the jetty to the lighthouse, or turn left to return to the Old Harbour, passing the Mosque of the Janissaries.

Distance
2.5km

Time
2–3 hours including sightseeing

Start/End Point
Venetian Harbour
✚ 28B2

Lunch
Dinos (£££)
✉ Aktí Enóseas 3, Inner Harbour
☎ (28210) 41865

Left: *the Naval Museum in the Firkás Tower*
Below: *the Venetian harbour is a focal point of tourist activity in Chaniá*

What to see in Chaniá Province

CHÓRA SFAKÍON ✪✪

In the 16th century this was the largest town on the south coast, with a population of 3,000, but rebellions during the Turkish occupation left Chóra Sfakíon largely impoverished, and what remained of the town was destroyed by bombs in World War II. Today it is no more than a small resort and ferry port, its main appeal the setting between the mountains and the crystal clear waters of the Libyan Sea. The small pebble beach is not ideal but you can take boats or walk to Sweetwater Beach, which takes its name from the freshwater springs seeping from beneath the rocks. The beach is a popular spot for nudist campers.

In high season the seaside tavernas of Chóra Sfakíon cater for boatloads of hungry hikers coming from the Samariá Gorge, waiting for buses back to Chaniá. The town has always been the capital of this mountainous, remote region and Sfakiots, as the locals are known, are traditionally a proud and independent people. The region was a centre of resistance during the fight for Cretan independence and continued this heroic tradition in World War II, sheltering Allied troops after the Battle of Crete.

ELAFONÍSI ✪✪✪

The semi-tropical beach of Elafonísi is one of the finest in the whole of Crete, with its pink-tinged sands and vivid turquoise waters. The beach is remotely located in the southwest of the island and visitors who wish to reach it by car face a long drive and many hairpin bends.

However, it is no longer the undiscovered and idyllic haven it used to be – there are now several restaurants, two small hotels, rooms to rent and, in high season, tourist boats and buses crammed full with eager daytrippers. A more peaceful alternative to the main beach is the tiny island of Elafonísi, just offshore, which is reached by wading knee-deep through the turquoise waters. Here there is another idyllic beach, where the waters are clear, shallow and ideal for children.

🔲 28B2
✉ 67km south of Chaniá
🍴 Seafront tavernas (£–££)
🚌 Service to Chaniá and Plakiás
⛴ Ferries to Agía Rouméli (Samariá Gorge), Soúgia, Palaióchora and the island of Gávdos.
♿ Few
↔ Loutró (➤ 88), Frangokástello (➤ 82), Fárangi Imbrotiko (➤ 82)

Fishing boats are a familiar sight on Crete's southwest coast

🔲 28A2
✉ 6km south of Chrysoskalítissas
🍴 Several cafés and tavernas (£–££)
🚌 Once a day from Chaniá
⛴ Ferries from Palaiókhora
♿ None
↔ Moní Chrysoskalítissas (➤ 88)

FALÁSARNA ✪✪✪

As you wind down the hillside to the west coast, Falásarna's magnificent sweeping beach comes into view, its crescent of pale sands, lapped by azure waters, stretching round to Cape Koutrí in the north.

Falásarna is also the site of an ancient city, the remains of which can be seen 2km north of the beach. (Follow the track for 1.5km beyond the last building.) Among the scattered remnants of the Hellenistic city-state are a 'throne' carved out of the rock, tombs, quarries, towers, water cisterns and the ruins of houses and storerooms. The remains centre around the harbour basin, its location some 100m inland showing clear evidence of the gradual shifting of the island. In the distant past Crete's west coast was uplifted by 6–9m, while parts of eastern Crete were submerged, including the sunken city of Oloús (► 50). Excavations of the ancient city are still in the early stages, and only a small portion of the harbour has been unearthed.

More remains lie at the top of Cape Koutrí, site of the acropolis. Close by, the less appealing – but economically necessary – plastic greenhouses produce off-season vegetables for export to mainland Greece.

+ 28A2
✉ 8km northwest of Plátanos
🍴 2 tavernas above the beach (£–££)
🚌 2 per day from Chaniá
♿ None
💰 No charge to see the ruins
↔ Kastélli Kissámou (► 86)

Enjoy the white sand and crystal clear waters of Elafonísi

FARÁNGI ÍMBROU (IMPROS GORGE) ✪✪✪

North of Chóra Sfakíon, the Impros Gorge is a small-scale version of the famous Samariá Gorge (➤ 20, 83). Equally spectacular, with similar scenery, it is far more peaceful than Samariá. The gorge is about 8km long, and the walk takes from 2 to 3 hours, either uphill from the coast east of Chóra Sfakíon, or downhill from Impros village at the beginning of the gorge. At the end you either have to walk to Chóra Sfakíon, catch a bus or wait for a taxi in Komitádes. The walk can only be made between May and October since winter torrents render the gorge impassable.

FARÁNGI SAMARIÁS (SAMARIÁ GORGE) (➤ 20, TOP TEN)

FRAGKOKÁSTELO ✪✪✪

The great square fortress, formidable from a distance, is actually no more than a shell. It was built by the Venetians in 1340 in an attempt to subdue the rebellious Sfakiots and the pirates who were attacking Crete from the African coast. In 1770 the Sfakiot rebel leader, Daskaloyiánnis, was forced to surrender to the Turks here, and in 1828, during the Greek War of Independence, the Greek leader, Hatzimicháli Daliánis, along with several hundred Cretans, died defending the fort against the Turks. According to the locals, on the anniversary of the massacre in mid-May their ghosts appear at dawn and march around the walls.

Below the fortress there is excellent swimming and snorkelling from the long sandy beach, and there are tavernas, shops, rooms to rent and even a disco. Less crowded beaches lie to the east and west.

✚ 28B2
✉ 54km southeast of Chaniá
🍴 Café (£) in Impros
🚌 Service from Chaniá and Chóra Sfakíon
♿ Not suitable
🎟 Free
↔ Fragkokástelo (below), Loutró (➤ 88)
❓ Sturdy footwear and drinks recommended

✚ 28B2
✉ 17km east of Chóra Sfakíon
🍴 Several tavernas (£–££)
🚌 Limited service to Chóra Sfakíon and Plakiás
♿ None
🎟 Free
↔ Chóra Sfakíon (➤ 80)

Above: *the Venetian fort of Fragkokástelo has played an important role in Crete's history*

A Walk Through The Samariá Gorge

Start at the tourist pavilion at the head of the gorge. Hikers should come equipped with sturdy footwear, sunhat, sunscreen and refreshments (there are drinking points and streams along the gorge but no food).

Take the stairway known as the xilóskala *(wooden stairs) which drops steeply, descending 1,000m in the first 2km.*

The first landmark is the tiny Church of Ágios Nikólaos, shaded by pines and cypresses.

The path narrows as you reach the bottom of the gorge (4km from the start). In summer the river is reduced to a mere trickle.

The half-way point, and a good spot for a picnic, is the abandoned village of Samariá. The inhabitants were rehoused when the area became a national park. To the east of the gorge lies the small 14th-century Church of Óssia María, containing original frescoes. The church gave its name to the village and gorge.

Follow the narrowing trail between towering cliffs, crossing the river at various points. Continue walking until you see a small church on the left.

Beyond the sanctuary built by the Sfakiots, you can see ahead the famous *sideróportes* or Iron Gates. The corridor narrows to a mere 3m, the towering walls either side rising to 300m.

Beyond the gates, the path opens out and you walk down the valley to the coast.

At the old abandoned village of Agía Rouméli, a drinks kiosk is a welcome sight.

Continue to the modern coastal village of Ágía Rouméli where tavernas, the cool sea water and the ferry back to civilisation await.

Distance
16km

Time
5–7 hours
🕐 May to mid-Oct (mid-Apr to Oct weather permitting)

Start point:
Omalós Plain, 43km south of Chaniá
✚ 28B2
🚌 Service from Chaniá

End Point:
Agía Rouméli
✚ 28B2
🚢 Ferries to Chóra Sfakíon, where there are buses back to Chaniá. Check times of the last boats and buses. Guided tours available through any travel agent.

Lunch
Tavernas at the top of the gorge and in Agía Rouméli (£–££); a picnic is recommended for the gorge.

Hikers arriving at the last bridge at the southern end of the Samariá Gorge

83

Coastal & Island Boat Tours

The small islands around Crete offer a retreat from the busy tourist haunts. Some are only accessible by private vessel, others are easily reached in the summer by ferry or excursion.

Above: on Santorini, Oía clings to the cliffs above Ammoúdi

Below: ferries vie for the lucrative tourist trade

One of the most popular excursions in the east of Crete is the islet of Spinalógka, north of Ágios Nikólaos. There are no beaches here but an ancient Venetian stronghold, which played a significant role in Cretan history (➤ 51) and the ruins of a former leper colony.

To the South

Off the south coast, a 13km boat trip from Ierápetra, the island of Yaidhouronísi, otherwise known as Chrýsi (the Golden Island) has idyllic sandy beaches, clear shallow waters and a small forest of cedar trees. Also along the southern coast, ferries are the only link between villages such as Loutró and Agía Rouméli, which are inaccessible by road.

Those who are curious to see Europe's most southerly point can take a ferry from Chóra Sfakíon to the island of Gávdos in the Libyan Sea. This lies 48km offshore, and ferries take about three hours. In ancient times the island was known as Claudia, and according to one of many

varying legends, it was here that the nymph Calypso seduced Ulysses. In the 13th century the island had a population of 8,000 – today there are about 40 permanent residents, most of them farmers struggling to earn a living from the parched soil. The landscape is flat and unremarkable, but there are some fine beaches and the turquoise waters are delightful for bathing.

Islands of Legend

From Kastélli Kissámou (➤ 86) in the northwest of Crete, a boat leaves daily in summer for the islet of Gramvoúsa with its Venetian

fortress. From here the tour goes on to the lagoon of Balos, whose pristine sands and azure waters make for ideal bathing. The island of Diá, north of Irákleio (and under its flightpath) can be visited on daytrips from the capital or from Limín Chersonísou. The Frenchman Jacques Cousteau dived here in search of the lost kingdom of Atlantis and found a Minoan city instead. The day trip includes a barbeque on board the boat with free wine, swimming in clear waters and a chance to see the rare Cretan wild goat (*kri-kri*).

Distant Shores

For those who would like to go further afield there are full day trips to Santorini, one of the Cyclades islands lying north of Crete. This volcanic island erupted in 1400–1450 BC, and it has been suggested that it was this explosion which caused the destruction of the first Minoan palaces on Crete. Today Santorini is a strikingly beautiful island of whitewashed houses, volcanic cliffs and beaches of black volcanic sand. The large excursion boats which cover the route between Crete and the island are equipped with bars and restaurants, and during the return journey evening entertainment is provided. The sailing takes three hours each way.

Organised Tours

Several of the Cretan tour agencies organise boat trips along the coast, not just for sightseeing, but also stopping for swimming and snorkelling in quiet bays and coves. From Chaniá's Venetian harbour there are half-day trips in glass bottom boats, which enable travellers to see the underwater delights too; from Réthymno, fishing trips day or night and tours to Georgióupoli for fishing, lunch and possible dolphin-spotting; from Ágios Nikólaos, tours to Spinalógka or to beaches along the coast. For information on boats and ferries, ask at the local tourist office or any travel agency; alternatively go to the harbour where bill boards advertise excursions.

Top: *ferry boats berth beneath the Venetian fortress at Spinalogka*
Above: *locally caught fish are a welcome product of Crete's love affair with the sea*

Below: *Crete has always bred skilful sailors*

📍 28B1
✉ 48km south of Chóra Sfakíon
🍴 Limited choice (£)
🚢 Ferries from Palaióchora and Chóra Sfakíon
♿ None

GÁVDOS ✪

A remote island between Crete and the shores of northern Africa, Gávdos is the southernmost point in Europe. A few families eke out a living here and there are some rooms to rent and a couple of basic tavernas. The landscape is somewhat desolate and sunbaked, but for those prepared to walk there are some beautiful, unspoilt beaches. Ferries (which can take several hours if the seas are choppy) arrive at Karabe; from here you walk for half an hour to the nearest beach or climb for an hour up to Kastrí, the main village on the island. Sometimes visitors can get transport from locals meeting the ferries.

📍 28B2
✉ 22km west of Réthymno
🍴 Tavernas on the main square (£–££)
🚌 Service to Réthymno and Chaniá
♿ Few

GEORGIOÚPOLI ✪

This north coast resort was named in honour of Prince George, who became High Commissioner of Crete in 1898, after the Turks were forced to recognise the island's right to autonomy. The fishing village is now a well established resort, with hotels, rooms to rent and a huge sweep of beach, but despite ongoing construction, it is still a relatively peaceful and relaxed place. The eucalyptus trees which shade the large central square are watered by the River Almyróu, which flows into the sea at Georgioúpoli. To explore the river, its birdlife, crabs and turtles, you can hire pedaloes or canoes from the little chapel which sits at the end of the causeway. The sandy beach stretches for several kilometres to the east, but beyond the causeway, the strong currents make swimming conditions dangerous.

Right: the harbour at Kastélli Kissámou with views across to the Rodópou peninsula. Excursion boats depart daily

📍 28A2
✉ 40km west of Chaniá
🍴 Papadakis (£)
🚌 Services to Falásarna, Chóra Sfakíon, Chaniá and Palaióchora
♿ None
↔ Falásarna (▶ 81), Kolymvári (below), Rodópou peninsula (▶ 90)

KASTÉLLI KISSÁMOU ✪

Known simply as Kastélli, this is a pleasant coastal town, still retaining some of its Cretan character but offering little of architectural interest. Few tourists stay here but there are a couple of hotels and some rooms to rent, many of them by the beach. In the town's main square, the Archaiologikó Mouseío (Archaeological Museum) is closed indefinitely for restoration. The best places to eat are the tavernas on the seafront, where you can also sample the locally produced red wine.

KOLYMVÁRI AND MONÍ GONIÁS ★★

At the foot of the Rodópou peninsula, Kolymvári is a pleasantly unspoilt coastal village, where local life goes on undisturbed by the few tourists who stay here. The beach is pebbly but the waters are crystal clear and there are splendid views over the Gulf of Chaniá.

About 1km north of the village the Moní Goniás has a delightful coastal setting. Founded in 1618, it has been rebuilt several times but the Venetian influence can still be seen in some of the architectural features. The small church contains some wonderfully detailed little icons from the 17th century along the top of the iconostatis, as well as votive offerings and other treasures. The most precious icons, dating from the 15th century, are housed in the museum, along with reliquaries and vestments. If the church and museum are closed, ask one of the monks to show you round. He will probably also point out the Turkish cannon ball lodged in the rear wall of the church.

🞦 28A2
✉ 23km west of Chaniá
☎ (28240) 22518
🕐 Daily 7–2, 4–8 (shorter hours in winter)
🍴 Seafront fish tavernas (£–££) in Kolymvári
🚌 Service to Kolymvári from Chaniá and Kastélli Kissámous
♿ Few
💲 Inexpensive
↔ Máleme (➤ 88), Kastélli Kissámou (➤ 86), Rodópou peninsula (➤ 90)

Moní Chrysoskalítissas (Our Lady of the Gold Steps) stands like a citadel above the sea

---

✚ 28B2
✉ 5km west of Chóra Sfakíon
🍴 The Blue House (£)
🚢 Ferry service to Chóra Sfakíon and Agía Rouméli
♿ None
↔ Chóra Sfakíon (► 80)

LOUTRÓ ❂❂❂

The only way to get to this delightful, car-free village is on foot or by boat. It is a tiny, remote place, with white cubed houses squeezed between towering mountains and the Libyan sea. There are half a dozen tavernas, a simple hotel, rooms to rent and some villas, but the majority of visitors are daytrippers coming on ferries from Chóra Sfakíon and Agía Rouméli. The pebble beach is not ideal but you can bathe from the rocks or hire canoes to explore offshore islets, coves and beaches. There are also boat trips to the sandy cove of Mármara and to Sweetwater Beach.

✚ 28A2
✉ 16km west of Chaniá
🍴 Several tavernas (£–££)
♿ Few
↔ Kolymvári (► 87), Rodoúpou peninsula (► 90)

MÁLEME ❂

The resort of Máleme is part of the long ribbon of modern development west of Chaniá. But it is for its role in World War II that this part of the coast is best known. It was at the Máleme airstrip that the Germans first landed in their invasion of 1941, the Allied forces retreating from 'Hill 107' above the airstrip. The Germans occupied this strategic target – but not without casualties. Today 'Hill 107' is the location of the German War Cemetery, where nearly 4,500 Germans are buried.

✚ 28A2
✉ 13km southwest of Váthi
☎ (28220) 61261
🕐 7AM–sunset
🍴 2 tavernas (£) on the Váthi road
♿ None
✋ Free
↔ Elafonísi (► 80)

MONÍ CHRYSOSKALÍTISSAS ❂❂

In a remote location at the southwest tip of the island, the whitewashed nunnery perches on a promontory above the sea. It was founded in a cave in the 13th century, but the present building dates from the mid-19th century and contains little of interest to the average tourist. Of the 200 sisters who used to live here, just one and a monk remain. For centuries Moní Chrysoskalítissas, its barrel roof a distinctive landmark, was a refuge for victims of shipwrecks on this remote and treacherous coast. The name 'Chrysoskalítissas' means 'Golden Steps', and was taken from the stairway of 90 steps leading from the nunnery down to the sea. According to legend, one of the steps is made of pure gold – but is only recognisable to those who are free of sin!

Many older women wear traditional black

PALAIÓCHORA ✪✪✪

Formerly a fishing village, and one-time haunt of hippies, Palaiochora now has universal appeal, with its fine setting below rugged mountains, its excellent beaches and relaxed atmosphere. As yet it is free from mass tourism, sitting on a small peninsula, crowned by the stone walls of a Venetian castle. Beneath it are two beautiful bays: to the east a sheltered but shingle and pebble beach, to the west a long stretch of wide golden sands shaded by tamarisk trees and very popular with windsurfers.

Venizélos, the main street, is particularly lively at night, when the road is closed to traffic and taverna tables spill out on to the pavements. Despite its popularity the centre has not lost all its Cretan character – locals still frequent the cafés and fishermen land their catch at the quayside. Linked to coastal villages by a regular ferry service, the resort makes an excellent base for exploring southern Crete, and is well placed for hikers, with coastal and mountain walks. There are also weekend boats to the tiny island of Gávdos (➤ 84, 86).

🔢 28A2
✉ 80km southwest of Chaniá
🍴 Tavernas along Venizélou (£–££)
🚌 Regular service to Chaniá
⛴ Ferries to Soúgia, Ágia Rouméli, Loutró, Chóra Sfakíon and Gávdos
☎ (028230) 41507
♿ Few
↔ Soúgia (➤ 91)

Below: Palaiochora is a pleasantly relaxed place, unspoilt by mass tourism

RODÓPOU PENINSULA ✪✪

The remote and rugged Rodópou peninsula extends 18km from the low lying coast west of Chaniá. The roads only go as far as the hamlet of Afráta and the main village of Rodópou. Beyond this the peninsula is uninhabited, the access limited to rough tracks and footpaths. There are good walks in the mountainous interior, but the tracks can be rough and there is very little shade. At the northeastern tip of the peninsula lie the scant Graeco-Roman remains of the Sanctuary of the goddess Diktynna, excavated by the Germans during World War II. Statues from the temple, which were discovered here, are now in the Chaniá Archaeological Museum (► 77). The easiest way to reach the remains is to take a boat excursion from Chaniá or Kolymvári. Part of the attraction is the pretty, sheltered cove below the sanctuary, ideal for swimming. Going by car entails a rough ride and half an hour's walk. On the west coast, the isolated little Church of Ágios Ioánnis is reached by a rough, dusty track from Rodópou, taking two to three hours. This is the route taken by thousands of pilgrims every year on 28 and 29 August (St John the Baptist's Day) to witness the baptism of boys with the name of John (Ioánnis).

SOÚDA BAY ALLIED WAR CEMETERY ✪✪

Sheltered by the Akrotíri peninsula to the north, Soúda Bay is Crete's largest natural harbour. Laid out on a neatly tended lawn, sloping down to the water, are the graves of 1,497 Allied soldiers who died defending Crete in World War II. The names of the soldiers, many of whom lie in unknown graves, are listed in the Cemetery Register, which is kept in a box at the entrance to the building. Of the total Allied force on the island of 32,000 men, 18,000 were evacuated, 12,000 were taken prisoner and 2,000 were killed.

Right: *the mountainous and uninhabited Rodópou peninsula, looking towards the town of Kastélli Kissámou*

The modern Church of Soúgia was built over the foundations of an early Christian basilica
Below: turquoise-blue waters in Soúgia Bay

SOÚGIA ✪✪

Set against the backdrop of the Samariá hills, this former fishing port is rapidly expanding into a tourist resort. Remotely located at the end of a long twisting road from Chaniá, it was first discovered by backpackers, but more and more tourists are coming for the long pebble beach, translucent blue waters, simple tavernas and coastal and mountain walks. As yet, accommodation is fairly basic. Just to the east of the Soúganos River mouth, a few Roman relics survive from the ancient port, which served the Graeco-Roman city of Elirós, 5km to the north. To the west a fine Byzantine mosaic, now in the Chaniá Archaeological Museum (► 77), was discovered where the modern church stands. Three kilometres to the west of the village, reached by a local boat or on foot over the cliffs (70–90 minutes) lie the classical Greek and Roman ruins of the ancient city of Lissós.

➕ 28A2
✉ 70km southwest of Chaniá
🍴 Simple tavernas in the resort (£)
🚌 Service from Chaniá
♿ None
🔁 Palaióchora (► 89)

Around the Akrotíri Peninsula

Distance
45 km

Time
Half a day, including
sightseeing

Start/End point
Chaniá
✚ 28B2

Lunch
Kalathás (£–££)
✉ Kalathás beach, Kalathás
☎ (28210) 64729

From Chaniá take the airport road, turning left at the top of the hill for the Venizélos Graves.

Stone slabs mark the graves of Elefthérios Venizélos (1864–1936), Crete's famous statesman and his son, Sophoklís. The site commands a magnificent view of Chaniá, mountains and coast.

Continue on the airport road, then follow signs for Agía Triáda.

The Venetian-influenced 17th-century monastery has a church with a fine Renaissance façade, and a peaceful courtyard where cats doze under fruit trees. A small shop sells olive oil made by the monks and a museum houses a collection of icons, reliquaries and vestments.

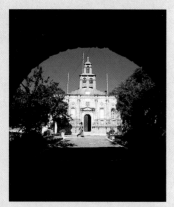

From Agía Triáda, walk or drive along the track through rocky, barren hills to the Gouvernétou Monastery (4.5km).

This sleepy, isolated monastery, founded in 1548, also shows a strong Venetian influence. From the monastery a path (about 30 minutes' walk) leads down to a beautiful gorge with the ruins of Katholikó Monastery and Cave of St John the Hermit. Pilgrims come here on 7 October each year to celebrate the saint's day.

The façade of peaceful Moní Gouvernétou, one of three monasteries on the Akrotíri peninsula

Retrace the route to Agía Triáda, go back towards the airport and after nearly 16km turn right for Chorafákeia (3km). At the village turn right for Stavrós.

The beautiful circular bay of pale sands and calm, aquamarine waters provided the setting for the final scenes in the film *Zorba the Greek*.

Return to Chorafákeia and in the village turn right for Chaniá. Reaching the coast, stop at Kalathás Beach.

One of the prettiest beaches on the peninsula, this is a good spot for a swim and a meal in a taverna before the return journey to Chaniá.

Where To...

Above: *Cretan oranges on a market stall*
Right: *on the waterfront in Siteía*

Irákleio & Lasíthiou

Prices

Approximate prices for a three-course meal for one without drinks and service:

£ = under €8
££ = €8–€15
£££ = above €15

Olive Oil

Foreigners often complain about the liberal use of olive oil in the local cooking. However, since the revelation that Crete has the lowest rate of heart disease and cancer in Europe, more and more tourists are showing an interest in the local diet.

Irákleio Town

Ionia (££)

Slightly off the tourist tract near the market, this restaurant dates from 1923 and is possibly the oldest on the island. Don't be put off by the non-descript decor. Locals come here regularly for the good selection of fresh Greek dishes. Try the snails with artichokes.

✉ Odós Evans 3 ☎ (2810) 283213 🕘 Mon–Fri 7AM–9:30PM, Sat 7–4

Kirkor (£)

The speciality of this café overlooking the Morozíni Fountain is *bougátsa*, the calorific, creamy custard pastry, liberally sprinkled with icing sugar.

✉ Plateía Venizélos ☎ (2810) 284295 🕘 Mon–Fri (some Sats) 5:30AM–11PM

Kyriakos (£££)

When locals want to impress their guests, they take them to Kyriakos, long considered Irákleio's best restaurant. There is outdoor seating as well as a dining room, the formal atmosphere softened by lush plants and friendly service. Simply, but beautifully prepared dishes. Reservations essential.

✉ Odós Dimokratías 45 ☎ (2810) 224649 🕘 Daily lunch and dinner

La Grande Trattoria (££–£££)

Comparatively smart taverna with candlelit interior on two floors. Extensive menu, focusing on pastas, pizzas and Italian specialities with a creative, international flare.

✉ Kórai 6 ☎ (2810) 300225 🕘 Daily lunch and dinner

Loúkoulos (£££)

An elegant restaurant on one of Irákleio's prettiest streets, which lures fashionable young locals as well as tourists. The food is Mediterranean with the emphasis on pastas and pizzas. Imaginative, very generous salads and delicious bread, baked in the wood oven.

✉ Odós Kórai 5, Irákleio ☎ (2810) 224435 🕘 Mon–Sat lunch and dinner

Pagopeion (££)

Popular spot in a pretty setting on Ágios Títos square. An old ice factory (*pagopeion* in Greek), it has been converted to a stylish restaurant/café/bar serving breakfast, lunch and dinner. Live or disco music is played until the early hours.

✉ Plateía Ágios Títos ☎ (2810) 246028 🕘 Daily 10:30AM–3 or 4AM

Tartuffo (£–££)

For those who want a change from Greek tavernas it is worth the 10-minute walk from the centre of town to this Italian restaurant. The distinctive wood-oven baked pizzas are particularly popular.

✉ Leofóros Dimokratías 83 ☎ (2810) 222103 🕘 Daily, dinner only

Tou Terzaki (££)

This restaurant near the tiny church of Ágios Demétrios is popular with the local smart set for its intimate ambience. Familiar Greek menu but made using quality, organic ingredients.

✉ Odós Marineli 17 ☎ (2810) 221444 🕘 Mon–Sat 5PM–1AM

Irákleio Province

Faistós
Ágios Ioánnis (£)
Inviting roadside taverna with tables in the garden. Good homemade fare; the speciality of charcoal-grilled rabbit is particularly recommended.

✉ **Mátala Road, Faistós** ☎ **(28920) 31560** ⏲ **Daily 11–10**

Fódele
El Greco (£)
Pretty setting in the village which, according to the locals, was the birthplace of Doménico Theotokópoulos, but known through history as El Greco. The emphasis is on meat, with lamb and chicken on the spit.

✉ **Fódele** ☎ **(28150) 21203** ⏲ **Daily 11–3, 6–10. Weekends only in winter.**

Mália
Petros (££)
The most pleasant place to eat in Mália is away from the bustling resort in the old town. Petros is one of the several tavernas set on the village square beside the church, and serves solid Greek fare such as *stifado* (beef in tomato sauce).

✉ **Plateia Agiou Dhimitríou, Mália** ☎ **(28970) 31887** ⏲ **Daily 5–11PM**

Mátala
Lions Restaurant (££)
Although this is one of several tavernas with an inviting setting right on Mátala beach, Lions' menu is more varied than most. Fresh seafoood takes top billing, but dishes like sole stuffed with crabmeat have an international flare. There is also an upstairs open-air bar for drinks and snacks.

✉ **Mátala** ☎ **(28920) 45108** ⏲ **Daily 9AM–late**

Skala (££)
You'll find this popular, family-run taverna at the far end of the waterfront, set on top of the rocks with wonderful views across the beach. There's fresh fish on the menu and open-air dining on the pretty terrace. A great place to relax and unwind.

✉ **Mátala** ☎ **(28920) 45489** ⏲ **Daily 10AM–late**

Lasíthiou Province

Ágios Nikólaos
Aouas Taverna (££)
Not as overtly tourist-orientated as the harbour and lakeside restaurants, and better value. Starters range from octopus with oregano to snails and fried courgette balls. Follow these with charcoal-grilled meats or the daily 'special'. Attractive trellised courtyard with trees and potted plants.

✉ **Odós Paleólogou** ☎ **(28410) 23231** ⏲ **Daily. Closed out of season**

Ariadne (£££)
This relatively expensive restaurant is on the east side of the harbour, one of the best in a scrum of eating places. Justly popular, it is run by a friendly family whose cooking raises the fairly plain menu above the ordinary. Eat later rather than earlier to enjoy the atmosphere.

✉ **Akti Koundoúrou** ☎ **(28410) 22658** ⏲ **Daily 12–11 in season**

Starters and Mains
If the starters look more varied and appetising than the main courses (as is often the case in Greek tavernas), there is nothing to stop you ordering two of these and skipping the main course altogether.

Lasíthiou

Kafeníon
Every village on Crete has a *kafeníon*, the traditional Greek coffee-house where local men play *távli* (backgammon) or cards, discuss politics, exchange gossip and watch the world go by. The coffee they drink is known locally as Greek and elsewhere as Turkish – that is, thick, black and sweet, and served in tiny cups. If you don't have a sweet tooth ask for *skéto* (without sugar) or *métrio* (medium sweet). Due to tourist demand instant coffee is now also available in most cafés.

Itanos (££)
Close to Plateía Venizélos, up from the port, this makes a welcome change from the more commercialised restaurants around the waterfront. Locals come for genuine Cretan fare and wine from the barrel. Tables on a terrace over the road.
✉ Odós Kyprou, 1 ☎ (28410) 25340 🕐 Daily 10AM–10PM but lunchtime is best

La Casa (£–££)
This lakeside café/restaurant is as popular for its central location as for its simple fare, from spinach pies to *souvlaki* (meat cooked on a skewer).
✉ Odós 28 Oktovriou 31 ☎ (28410) 26362 🕐 Daily 9AM–midnight

Pelagos (£££)
Save this for a special occasion. It is Agíos Nicólaos' smartest taverna, set in a neo-classical building with a large courtyard shaded by palms. The emphasis is on fish and seafood.
✉ Odós Koráka 9 ☎ (28410) 25737 🕐 Apr–Oct daily noon–midnight

Eloúnta
Ferryman Taverna (££)
This waterside restaurant takes its name from the old BBC television series, *Who Pays the Ferryman?*, which was filmed at nearby locations. The Cretan menu is a cut above the usual fare, with more elaborate dishes such as pork cooked with bacon, mushrooms and garlic in a wine sauce. Try rusk-like Cretan bread.
✉ Waterfront, Eloúnta ☎ (28410) 41230 🕐 Apr–Oct daily 10AM–late

Ierápetra
Castello (££)
One of the several tavernas along the waterfront by the old town, this one will grab you for the delicious smells of fish and meat cooking on its outdoor grill. But first try the starters, homemade daily by the owner's mother.
✉ Stratigou Samovil, Ierápetra ☎ (28420) 22424 🕐 Daily 10:30AM–1AM

Káto Zákros
Maria (£)
Simple fish taverna on a delightful pebble beach, near the Minoan remains of Zákros Palace. Fresh fish such as bream, snappers and mullet are available unless the *Meltémi* wind blows. The geese on the beach are very much part of the establishment (but not the menu).
✉ Káto Zákros, Siteía ☎ (28430) 93316 🕐 Mid-Mar to end Jun, Sep–Oct Tue–Sun 8–3; Jul–Aug 8–6 daily

Makrygialos
Faros (££)
Fresh fish is assured at this friendly waterfront restaurant, run by a family of fishermen for nearly 40 years. There are outdoor and indoor tables, while the little bar next door is decorated with old family photos and memorabilia.
✉ Waterfront, Makrygialos ☎ (28430) 52456 🕐 Daily lunch and dinner

Kavos (££)
The fresh seafood and homemade Cretan specialities change daily at this taverna by the waterfront. It has its own bakery, and the excellent

wine comes from the grandfather's vineyard in a nearby village. There are outdoor tables beside the beach, and a glass-enclosed balcony for windy nights.

✉ Waterfront, Makrygialos
☎ (28430) 51325 🕐 Daily
lunch and dinner

Mochlos
Restaurant Kavouria (££)
This waterside taverna overlooks a sandy cove, its bright blue and green wooden tables and chairs matching the colours of the ocean. A good range of Greek dishes and fresh fish complement the beautiful views.

✉ Waterfront, Mochlos
☎ (28430) 94204 🕐 Daily
luch and dinner

Palaikastro
Elena (£)
Next to the tourist office, this is a taverna of great character, offering Cretan specialities such as rabbit cooked in wine, *briam* (aubergines and courgettes), cheese pies and stuffed vine leaves. Wine comes from the barrel and there are homemade sweets and ice creams.

✉ Palaikastro ☎ (28430)
61234 🕐 Apr–Oct daily mid-
morning to 11PM

Siteia
Cretan House (££)
The large outdoor terrace is set right along thye waterfront near the beach. The indoor restaurant is charmingly decorated with a re-creation of a Cretan house. It serves good Greek and Cretan specialities and fresh fish.

✉ Odós Karamanli 10
☎ (28430) 25133 🕐 Daily
10AM–late

Mixos (££)
Set back from the harbour, this is where you'll find the locals dining out. Good-value Cretan dishes and charcoal-grilled fish and meat, with heady wine from the barrel to complement the food.

✉ Odós Vinzétzos Kornárou
117 ☎ (28430) 22416 🕐 Daily
10AM–late

Ágios Konstantínos, Lasíthiou Plateau
Díkti (£)
Unpretentious roadside café in a small Lasíthiou Plateau village. The menu is written on a board and includes roast meats, moussaka and salads. The owners also sell the embroidery and linen that can be seen fluttering outside.

✉ Ágios Konstantínos,
Lasíthiou ☎ (28440) 31255
🕐 Daily 8AM–6PM. Closed winter

Tzermiádho, Lasíthiou Plateau
Kronio (£)
This is the oldest restaurant on the plateau, established before the advent of tourism. Authentic Greek fare includes *stifado*, which is made fresh daily, lamb with white artichokes (spring only), *dolmades* and cuttle fish with spices. All dishes use fresh local produce. Delicious cheese and vegetable pies are served as starters or as a snack. The charming Vassilis and his French wife, Christine, encourage customers to take a good look in the kitchen before making their choice. The best time to do so is around noon.

✉ Tzermiádho, Lasíthiou
☎ (28440) 22375 🕐 Daily.
Closed winter

Tirópitta
A favourite snack among the Cretans are *tirópitta*, delicious hot pastries filled with feta cheese. Other readily available snacks are *souvlaki*, sweet pastries or salted nuts, pumpkin seeds and chick peas, sold from street carts.

Réthymno & Chaniá

Greek Cheeses

Crete has a variety of cheeses, including the ubiquitous feta, a white semi-soft salted cheese served with *khoriatíki* (Greek salad), the Cretan *myzíthra*, a ewe's milk cheese similar to ricotta, which comes either sweet or salted, and *graviéra*, a hard, sharp, yellow cheese.

Réthymno Town

Avli (£££)

It is well worth splashing out for a meal in this elegant restaurant within an old Venetian manor house. The menu features imaginative dishes such as baby lobster in shrimp sauce, lamb with greens in egg lemon sauce, and casseroled goat with traditional Cretan pilaf. The wine list is unusually varied and gives useful explanations of Cretan and Greek wines. Delightful courtyard for outdoor meals. Reservations are recommended.

✉ Odós Xanthoudídou 22
☎ (28310) 26213 🕐 Daily 11–3, 7–11

Kypia Maria (£)

Caged canaries provide the background music in this homely taverna, located in a secluded alley near the Rimondi Fountain. Customers choose their dishes from the kitchen where everything is home-made: *pastitsio*, stuffed aubergines, lamb in lemon sauce, pork and rabbit and a good choice of vegetable dishes. Before ordering dessert it is worth bearing in mind that after your meal, cheese pies and honey are on the house.

✉ Odós Moshovítou 20
☎ (28310) 29078 🕐 Mar–end Oct 10AM–11PM

O Goúnos (£)

In the old town, this is a lively place on summer evenings when the family play folk music. Wholesome home-cooking with Cretan specialities.

✉ Odós Koronaíou 6
☎ (28310) 28816 🕐 Daily, lunch and dinner

Othonas (£–££)

Overtly touristy, in the centre of the old town, but a great spot for people-watching. Steaks, pasta dishes and home-made sauces are the specialities, but there are numerous other international dishes to choose from. Lively, bustling atmosphere. Set menus available.

✉ Plateía Petiháki 27
☎ (28310) 55500 🕐 Daily, all day in season. Closed winter

Palazzo (£££)

Thanks to the enticing harbour setting and choice of delicious fresh fish and seafood, this is one of the most expensive restaurants in town. Save it for a special occasion and reserve a table on the rooftop.

✉ Réthymno Harbour
☎ (28310) 25681 🕐 Daily, lunch and dinner

Plateía Ktouloúmbasi (££)

Near the Hotel Ideon and close to the Venetian harbour, this taverna serves Greek and Cretan dishes, pizzas and other international fare. In summer tables are laid out across the road with views of the ferries from Piréaus.

✉ Plateía Plastíra 1, Réthymno
☎ (28310) 53598 🕐 Daily, lunch and dinner

La Rentzo (£££)

There is plenty of atmosphere in this splendid old Venetian interior. It is on the pricey side but it is quite smart and very friendly, and makes a good spot for a candlelit dinner. Tables are also laid outside in summer. International and Greek dishes including lamb in honey sauce. Good steaks. Order in advance for special dishes, especially for fresh fish.

✉ **Odós Radamanthous, 9** ☎ **(28310) 26780** 🕐 **May–Oct lunch and dinner; Nov–Apr dinner only 6–1**

Sunset Taverna (££)

This taverna lives up to its name, enjoying splendid sunsets from the west side of the Fortétza. Reliable Greek food, longer-than-average wine list and tables by the sea.

✉ **Periferiakos** ☎ **(28310) 23943** 🕐 **Apr–Oct daily, mid-morning to small hours**

Réthymno Province

Agía Galíni
Onar (££)

The main attraction here is the splendid harbour and sea views from the roof garden restaurant. Wide range of Greek dishes, as well as home-made pizzas, pasta, fresh fish. The restaurant is expanding to take over the ground floor.

✉ **Agía Galíni** ☎ **(28320) 91288** 🕐 **Easter–end Oct all day every day**

Chaniá Town

Akrogiáli (£)

A popular seafront taverna, highly sought after for its excellent value fish and seafood. It boasts a friendly and bustling atmosphere and reservations are recommended in season.

✉ **Akti Papanikolí, Néa Chora** ☎ **(28210) 73110** 🕐 **All year, noon to late evening**

Anaplous (£££)

Within the roofless ruins of a Turkish mansion, the Anaplous is a picturesque

spot for an evening dish of *mezedes* with *ouzo*, or a full Greek meal. Guitar music enlivens the ambience on occasional summer evenings.

✉ **Sífaka 34** ☎ **(28210) 41321** 🕐 **Daily 7PM–1AM**

Arti (£££)

A far cry from the basic Greek taverna, this is an elegant candlelit restaurant serving dishes such as thick fillet steaks, delicious salmon and lamb. It is professionally run by a Swiss and German husband and wife.

✉ **Skoufon 15** ☎ **(28210) 75867** 🕐 **Early Mar to mid-Oct 7PM–midnight**

Dinos (£££)

This is probably the best fish taverna in town, with a delightful harbourside setting overlooking the fishing boats and cruisers. Fresh fish, including lobster, is available daily (if it's frozen they say so on the menu). Try the mixed fish plate for two. Ask to see the lovely Venetian architectural features beyond the kitchen.

✉ **Akti Enóseos 3, Inner Harbour** ☎ **(28210) 41865** 🕐 **Daily 8AM–2AM (or later if customers are still here)**

Ela (££)

This atmospheric restaurant is set inside the ochre walls of a roofless Venetian building. The Cretan cuisine includes wonderful lamb and chicken dishes, steaks, fresh fish and vegetarian dishes such as *boureki*. There's a good range of wines and live music too.

✉ **Odós Kondilaki 47** ☎ **(28210) 74128** 🕐 **Daily lunch and dinner**

Dining Al Fresco

Greeks dine late (from 9PM) and enjoy sitting outside to eat – either on a street pavement, a taverna courtyard or a seaview terrace.

Extras

A service charge of 15 per cent is usually included in your bill. If you are particularly pleased with the service you can leave a little extra for the waiter.

Chánia

Tavernas and Restaurants

Eating establishments are normally called **tavernas** or **estiatória** (restaurants) and the difference between them is not very clear cut. These days tavernas range from no-frills family-run places with plastic tablecloths to smarter establishments catering primarily for tourists. **Estiatória** are traditional restaurants serving local dishes, usually more upmarket and expensive than tavernas and often with lovely surroundings. Meat-eaters will enjoy the **psistariá**, where chicken, lamb, pork, kebabs and other meats are barbecued over charcoal.

Esperides (£)

A friendly, family-run restaurant, the Esperides has a good choice of home-cooked vegetable starters (fried aubergine, *dolmades*, pumpkin balls), as well as meat and cheese pies, rabbit and other Greek dishes. Tables, all with fresh flowers, are laid out on the terrace and spill on to the pavement.

✉ **Odós Skoufon 20** ☎ **(28210) 93065** 🕐 **Apr–Oct lunch and dinner**

Nikterida (£££)

On the neck of the Akrotíri peninsula, a short taxi ride from Chaniá. A restaurant recommended by locals in the know, serving well prepared Cretan and other Mediterranean food. Garden with wonderful views across Soúda Bay. Good selection of wines. Occasionally there is traditional music, which is why it is used by tour companies as part of their Cretan evenings.

✉ **Korákies** ☎ **(28210) 64215**

Penaléon (££)

'The Hungry Man' is popular with locals and unlikely to be found by most visitors to Chaniá. On the outskirts of town, not far from the football stadium. Unusual food including some dishes with a Middle-Eastern influence. The restaurant sign is in Greek only – look for the sign showing a man about to eat with a napkin around his neck

✉ **Odós El Venizelou, 86** ☎ **(28210) 40325**

Semiramis (££)

On a pretty alley near the harbour, the taverna has a large terrace/garden, wide variety of home-made starters and good fillet steaks with a choice of seven different sauces. There is live music in the evenings.

✉ **Odós Skoufon, 8** ☎ **(28210) 98650** 🕐 **Daily 11AM–after midnight. Closed winter**

Suki Yaki (££)

Good Chinese and Thai cooking in a stylish restaurant next to the Archaeological Museum. The courtyard, where tables are laid in summer, overlooks the museum garden with its Turkish fountain.

✉ **Khalidon 28** ☎ **(28210) 74264** 🕐 **Daily 6PM–midnight**

Taman (££)

Converted from a part of the old Turkish baths, and serving Greek, Cretan, Turkish and Arabic specialities, this is one of Chánia's most popular haunts. The interior, below street level, has fairly basic décor but is candlelit and full of atmosphere. In summer the tables pack the pavement outside and there's usually live music at weekends. The house wine is served in a jug straight from the barrel.

✉ **Odós Zambelíou 49** ☎ **(28210) 96080** 🕐 **Daily 7PM–12:30AM (dinner only)**

Tholos (£££)

The evocative setting, within the ruins of a Victorian town house, combined with the quality of the Cretan meat dishes, makes this one of Chániá's most desirable tavernas.

✉ **Agia Deka 36** ☎ **(28210) 46725** 🕐 **Daily 12–12 in season**

Well of the Turk (££)

As the name suggests, this cellar restaurant has an eastern flavour, with spicy food and atmospheric Arabic music.

✉ Kaliníkou Zarpáki ☎ (28210) 54547 🕔 All year, except Tue, 6:30 until late. Open for lunch May–Sep

Chánia Province

Kalathás
Kalathás (£–££)

It is primarily the setting on a beautiful beach of the Akrotíri peninsula (➤ 92) that distinguishes this taverna. Fresh fish, including sea urchins, local whitebait and octopus are usually available, and the menu also features steak, *souvlaki* and other standard dishes. The perfect place for a lazy beach lunch.

✉ Kalathás Beach, Kalathás, Chaniá ☎ (28210) 64729 🕔 Late Mar–early Nov depending on weather; 8AM–5 or 6AM (closes 9PM in autumn).

Kastélli Kíssamou
Castelli Taverna (££)

On the ground floor of the Castelli Hotel. Good food in the very heart of town activity.

✉ Plateía Kastélliou ☎ (28220) 22140 🕔 Daily in season

Papadakis (£)

On the seafront, this is probably the best value taverna in Kastélli Kíssamou for fresh fish. Lobsters, sword fish, shrimps and baby squid are likely to be on the menu.

✉ Plateía Telonio ☎ (28220) 22340 🕔 Daily 8AM–late. Closed winter

Loutró
The Blue House (£)

The combination of the views over Loutró's harbour, the excellence of the seafood and Greek cuisine and the friendly atmosphere make this one of the most inviting restaurants on Chaniá's southern coastline. The only access is by foot or ferry (➤ 88). The Blue House is also a guest house, but Loutró is a very popular little port and you would be lucky to find a room available in season without booking well in advance.

✉ Loutró ☎ (28250) 91127 🕔 Apr–Oct daily 12–4 and 7–11. Ferries every three hours from Chóra Sfakíon in high season, two a day in low season.

Palaióchora
Dionysos (££)

One of many tavernas along the main street of this busy south coast resort, with tables spilling out on to the pavement. You can make your selection of the dishes from the kitchen in true Greek style.

✉ Vénizelos ☎ (28230) 41243 🕔 Daily 12–3, 5:30–12. Closed winter

Plataniás
Mylos (£££)

This popular taverna not only serves some of the best Cretan food in the area (particularly the excellent range of charcoal grilled meats) but also has a delightful garden setting complete with a watermill and duck pond.

✉ Plataniás, 12km west of Chaniá ☎ (28210) 68578 🕔 Daily dinner only. Closed winter

Raki

Be prepared for a complimentary glass of *rakí* (or *tsikoudiá*) at the end of your meal. This ubiquitous spirit, drunk neat in small glasses, is distilled from the skin and pips of grapes. Many Cretans drink it daily, and in winter it is taken with honey to provide relief from colds.

Irákleio

Prices

Expect to pay for a room per night in high season:

£   = under €35
££   = €35–73
£££   = over €73

Renting Rooms

All over Crete you will see signs for 'Rent Rooms'. These are graded from A to C and could be in an uninspiring modern block or a friendly private home. Accommodation in the latter is often more pleasant and a good deal cheaper than a room in a low category hotel. Discounts are normally given on stays of three nights or more.

Irákleio Town

Astoria Capsis Hotel (£££)

A very civilised and modern hotel close to the Archaeological Museum on the busy Elefthérias Square in the centre of Irákleio Town. There is some noise from the busy streets around the hotel, but it makes up for this with good facilities including a fourth-floor swimming pool with snack bar, main restaurant and ground floor Café Capsis. There are 117 air-conditioned rooms and 14 suites.

✉ Plateía Elefthérias
☎ (2810) 229002; fax: (2810) 229078

El Greco (££)

On a busy shopping street, this is one of the town's most central hotels. There are 90 rooms, of which most could best be described as adequate rather than spacious. The public rooms include a snack-bar, cafeteria and breakfast room. As is the case with all of the hotels in Irákleio Town, noise is one of the main drawbacks.

✉ 4 Odós 1821
☎ (2810) 281071; fax: (2810) 281702

Kronos Hotel (££)

The appearance of this modern block may be uninspiring, but don't be deceived, this is a friendly, family-run place with an excellent location, right on the seafront and with several tavernas nearby. Most rooms have sea view. Open all year.

✉ Corner of Sophokles Venizélou and Agarathou Streets ☎ (2810) 282240; fax: (2810) 285853

Lato (££)

A stylish, well-equipped hotel, close to the old port and Archaeological Museum, the Lato caters for both business and pleasure. Modern, soundproofed guest rooms come with TV, air conditioning, internet access, minibars and balcony; some overlook the fortress by the port. Book in advance as it is popular.

✉ Epimenidou 15 ☎ (2810) 228103; fax: (2810) 240350

Agia Pelagía

Sofitel Capsis Palace & Bungalows (£££)

One of Crete's largest and most luxurious complexes, set on a peninsula with sandy bays either side. The hotel comprises two main buildings and villa-like bungalows set among beautifully maintained gardens. Facilities include two sandy beaches, indoor and outdoor pools, watersports, fitness centre, shopping arcade, and even a zoo which includes the rare Cretan ibex. The Taverna Poseidon offers 30 different Greek *mezédes*, fresh local fish, music and wonderful views across the bay.

✉ Agía Pelagía ☎ (2810) 811212; fax: (2810) 811076
🚌 Regular service to Irákleio

Mátala

Hotel Zafiria (££)

Mátala's largest hotel has 70 rooms and is on the main road in the town centre. Rooms are simple, but all have a balcony facing either the sea or the hills inland. There is a hotel bar and restaurant.

✉ Mátala ☎ (2810) 45112; fax: (2810) 45725

Lasíthiou

Ágios Nikólaos

Elpida Hotel (££)

Well away from the bustle of Ágios Nikólaos, the hotel is set on a peaceful hillside overlooking sea and mountains. The two beaches of Kaló Khório are the best in the area – alternatively you can use the open-air pool. The hotel has a restaurant, lounge/bar, pool snack-bar, children's playground and games.

✉ Kaló Khório, PO Box 26, Ágios Nikólaos 721 00
☎ (28410) 61403; fax: (28410) 61481

Istron Bay Hotel (£££)

This secluded hotel, 13km east of Ágios Nikólaos, has a cliff-hanging setting above a glorious small bay. There are 145 sea-view rooms in local style, three restaurants (the hotel is well-known for its cuisine), open-air pool, tennis, beach bar, watersports, fishing trips and organised day and evening activities. Despite the size, it is family run and has a more friendly atmosphere than most hotels of its category.

✉ 721 00 Kaló Khório
☎ (28410) 61347; fax: (28410) 61383 🚌 Regular service to Ágios Nikólaos, Irákleio and Siteía

Minos Beach (£££)

Before the Eloúnta Beach was built this hotel enjoyed a reputation as the finest hotel on the island. Lying on a secluded promontory near the centre, it provides luxurious accommodation in the main block or bungalows, a good choice of watersports and swimming from rocky inlets, sandy beaches or the hotel's heated outdoor pool. The equally luxurious Minos Palace nearby is owned by the same company.

✉ Ágios Nikólaos 72100
☎ (28410) 22345; fax: (28410) 22548

Sgouros Hotel (£)

The main advantage of this modern hotel is its location by the beach. There is no restaurant attached to the hotel, but plenty of tavernas nearby or in the centre.

✉ Kitroplatia, Ágios Nikólaos
☎ (28410) 28931; fax (28410) 25568

Eloúnta Beach Hotel (£££)

A member of the Leading Hotels of the World group, this is generally recognised as the most exclusive resort hotel in Greece. The roll call of VIP guests includes prime ministers and presidents . The rooms, bungalows and suites have bay or garden views, marble bathrooms, TVs, bathrobes and fresh flowers. Among the amenities are three restaurants (Italian, Greek and International cuisine), a private sandy beach, heated outdoor pool, health and fitness centre, floodlit tennis courts, watersports centre and limousine and heli-pad.

✉ 72 053 Eloúnta ☎ (28410) 41412/3; fax: (28410) 41373

Palaíkastro

Hotel Hellas (£)

This modest and very inexpensive family-run hotel lies in the centre of the village. The restaurant/café, with good-value food, is popular with locals.

✉ Palaikastro ☎ (28430) 61240 🚌 Services to Siteía, Vái and Káto Zákros

Hot and Cold

Don't be surprised if hot water is in short supply. Many properties in Greece have solar-powered heating systems and cloudy weather may mean short supplies. Some places may have a back-up electrical system to cover for bad weather.

Réthymno & Chaniá

Prices
Hotel prices, which vary according to the season, are strictly controlled by the government. Off-season there are normally substantial discounts on the official rates. In high season, however, you may be hit by hidden extras such as surcharges for air conditioning or a stay of less than three nights.

Réthymno Town
Fortezza (££)
Centrally located, and close to the old fort, this stylish hotel in the centre of town has its own swimming pool and garden courtyard. All rooms have air conditioning and balconies.

✉ Odós Melissinou 16
☎ (28310) 55551; fax: (28310) 54073

Grecotel Rithymna Beach Hotel and Bungalows (£££)
On the beach 7km northeast of Réthymno, this huge luxury complex is highly popular with families. Altogether there are around 600 rooms, some in the main hotel buildings, others in bungalows and villas. The range of amenities includes restaurants, pools, watersports and fitness club and there is plenty on offer for children, including supervised camping on the beach.

✉ Adele Beach, Réthymno
☎ (28310) 71002; fax: (28310) 71668

Hotel Leo (£)
This 500-year-old house, which used to belong to a wealthy Venetian, has 11 simple rooms, all with shower, and its own café/bar. It lies in the heart of the old town and preserves its Venetian character.

✉ Odós Vafe 2 ☎ (28310) 29958

Ideon (££)
Good value hotel, well placed for the centre of the city and the Venetian harbour. Built in the 1970s, it offers 95 modern rooms with air-conditioning, a swimming pool and a restaurant.

✉ Plateía Plastíra 10
☎ (28310) 28667; fax: (28310) 28670

Minos Mare (£££)
Large, modern hotel standing on the sand and shingle beach of Platanias, 5km from Réthymno. Ideal for all ages, with pools, gym, sauna, evening entertainment and children's facilities. Guests can also use the facilities of the sister hotel, the Minos, 3km away.

✉ Platanias, Réthymno
☎ (28310) 50388; fax (28310) 53310

Agía Galíni
Hotel Leto (£)
This is a small family hotel in a pretty residential street very close to the centre and harbour. There are ten simple, clean rooms, all with private bathrooms.

✉ Agía Galíni, Réthymno
☎ (28320) 91231

Plakiás
Neos Alianthos (££)
Family-run, informal hotel across the road from the beach of Plakiás. The hotel has 94 bedrooms on two floors and an outdoor freshwater pool. Plakiás' shops, bars and tavernas are a few minutes' walk away.

✉ Plakiás, Réthymno
☎ (28320) 31280; fax: (28320) 31282

Chaniá Town
Amphora (££)
A prime location on the Venetian harbour and beautifully renovated rooms within an historic house make this one of the most desirable central hotels of Chaniá. The building is partly Venetian, partly

Turkish and every room is different. Breakfasts of various cheeses, cheeses, ham, fruit and home-made jams. The hotel has a harbourside restaurant.

✉ **Odós Parados Theotokopoúlou 2** ☎ **(28210) 93224; fax: (28210) 93226**

Contessa (££)

On a narrow street in the Venetian quarter, with views of the harbour, this is a charming old-fashioned guest house. There are only six bedrooms, and you would need to book in advance for the high season.

✉ **Theofanous 15** ☎ **(28210) 98565 (also fax)**

Doge Apartments (££)

This old Venetian house, just up the street from the port, has been converted into eight fully equipped apartments for two to five people.

✉ **Odós Kondilaki 14–16** ☎ **(28210) 95466; fax: (28210) 96020**

Hotel Doma (££)

Only 20 minutes from the centre of Chaniá, on the coastal road, the hotel occupies a handsome neo-classical house which was formerly the British Consulate. Furnished with antiques and prints, it still retains a traditional feel. There is no official restaurant but the top-floor breakfast room also serves as a snack bar at other times of day.

✉ **Elefthérios Venizélos 124** ☎ **(28210) 51772; fax: (28210) 41578** 🚌 **Regular service to central Chaniá**

Halépa (££)

Located in the elegant quarter of Khalépa, the house was built in the 19th century and was formerly used as the British Embassy. It has 46 air-conditioned rooms (many with sea views), a dining room, palm-tree garden and panoramic sun terrace.

✉ **Elefthérios Venizélos 164** ☎ **(28210) 28440; fax: (28210) 28439** 🚌 **Regular service to central Chaniá**

Nostos (£)

Delightful bed-and-breakfast in a converted Venetian house on one of Chaniá's prettiest alleys. Some rooms have sea views.

✉ **Zambelioú 42-46** ☎ **(28210) 94743; fax: (28210) 54502**

Loutró

Porto Loutró (££)

The only way you can get to this charming little hotel, set on Loutró's bay, is by boat or on foot. The best rooms are at the top, and they have roof terraces.

✉ **Loutró, Chora Sfakíon, Chaniá** ☎ **(28250) 91433; fax (28250) 91091** 🚤 **Regular boat from Agía Roúmeli and Chóra Sfakíon.**

Vlatos Kissámou

Milia (£–££)

High season here is the winter when log fires burn and guests are plied with free *rakí* and hot chestnuts. This is alternative Crete, idyllic for nature lovers and a far cry from the tourist fleshpots of the coast. The village has 12 rustic stone dwellings, lit by oil lamps (no electricity) and supplied with organic food from the land – rabbits, chickens, lambs, honey and wine.

✉ **Milia, Vlatos Kissámou** ☎ **(28210) 46774**

Hotel Stars

Greek hotels are currently classified into six grades, starting with deluxe (L) and going down from Category A through to the very basic Category E. A list of hotels on Crete is available from overseas offices of the Greek National Tourist Organisation (known as the EOT or GNTO).

Markets

When and Where

Shop opening hours vary widely according to the place and season. Officially shops open on Monday, Wednesday and Saturday from 8 or 9AM–1:30 or 2PM, and on Tuesday, Thursday and Friday the same hours, but reopening from 5 or 5:30PM–8 or 8:30PM. Shops for tourists, however, tend to be open all day seven days a week, often until 10PM or 11PM. The largest concentration of shops are in Irákleio, Réthymno, Chaniá and Ágios Nikólaos.

Irákleio Open Air Market

A stroll along Odós 1866 any morning of the week will give you an idea of the wealth of produce from Crete's fertile valleys and hothouses. Bustling, colourful and crowded, the market retains some of the flavour of the former oriental bazaar under the Turks and Venetians. Stalls are piled high with fresh fruit and vegetables: peppers, aubergines, beans, zucchini, peaches, cherries and melons – to name just a few. Butchers shops are hung with whole carcasses and strings of sausages, leather stalls with bags and belts, small shops with brightly woven rugs and embroidered linen. Grocery shops and stalls are crammed with baskets of spices, jars of wild herb honey, Cretan mountain tea, olives and nuts, goat and sheep's cheeses. As well as culinary delights there are souvenirs such as sponges and Cretan knives, and everyday goods such as wooden spoons, copper coffee pots, knives or hand-made leather boots. Having soaked up the atmosphere and struck your bargains, sit at the café of the Turkish pumphouse in Plateía Kornarou at the end of the street or one of the small tavernas in the side street to the east where many of the marketholders take their meals.

✉ **Odós 1866, Irákleio**
🕐 **Mon, Wed, Sat 8–2, Tue, Thu, Fri 8–2, 5–8:30**

Chaniá Market

The splendid market hall, which provides a cool retreat from the street in summer, was built in 1911. Cruciform in shape, it was designed on the lines of the marketplace in Marseilles. The spectacle of herbs and honeys, oils and spices, dried fruits, cheese, fish, meat, fruit and vegetables is every bit as alluring and lively as the market in Irákleio. This is the perfect place to buy your picnic or beach snack: pastries filled with feta cheese or wild greens, sweet tomatoes, olives, peaches, figs and bottles of Cretan wine. Be sure to try the cheeses before you buy. Stallholders will encourage you to taste each variety and tell you where they are made. In the non-edible line, a local and very distinctive speciality which you can fine here in all sizes is *koulouri* – the dried, elaborately decorated Cretan wedding bread. These are handmade from real dough, and are said to bring luck to wedded couples – alternatively they are taken home by tourists as souvenirs. Insect repellent, applied every three months, preserves the bread.

✉ **Plateía Sophokles Venizélos** 🕐 **Mon, Wed, Thu, Sat 8–2, Tue, Fri 8:30–1:30, 5–8 (summer 6–9)**

Other Markets

Irákleio also has a Saturday morning market by the port. This is less atmospheric than the town's street market, but sells a wide variety of goods including food and clothes. Other main towns such as Réthymno, Ágios Nikólaos and Siteía have markets during the week, but on a small scale beside those of Irákleio and Chaniá.

Arts, Crafts & Antiques

Jewellery
The main towns offer a wide choice of gold and silver jewellery, some of it very stylish. There are also some beautiful reproductions of Minoan jewellery wrought in gold and other metals. In Irákleio, Dedhálou is the best source for good-quality jewellery.

Worry Beads
Greeks fiddle with worry beads or *kombolói* as a way of relaxing. These are often bought as souvenirs, from tourist shops, markets or jewellers.

Wines and Spirits
You never have to go far to find a shop selling Greek wines and spirits. Crete produces its own wine (red and white) *retsina* (resinated wine) and *rakí* (spirit). You can also buy cheap Greek brandy and *ouzo*, an aniseed-flavoured spirit similar to Pernod.

Irákleio Province

Irákleio Town

Diktamos
This small, cheerful shop sells a wide range of natural Cretan products, from soaps and sponges to comb honey and spices. Local wine, *raki* and herbed olive oils are presented in decorative glass bottles.
✉ **Museum Square** ☎ **(2810) 226186** 🕒 **Daily 9–7**

Helen Kastrinoyanni
Opposite the Archaeological Museum, Helen Kastrinoyanni's shop specialises in Cretan handwoven embroideries, rugs, woven linen, jewellery and reproductions of clay figurines which you may well recognise if you have already visited the museum.
✉ **Plateía Elefthérias 1** ☎ **(2810) 226186** 🕒 **Summer Mon–Sat 8:30–7:30, Sun 11–7; winter shorter hours. Closed Sun**

Moustakis
High quality leather shoes and boots for men and women. Although the stock is made in Greece, it is not cheap.
✉ **Odós Daidalos 3** ☎ **(2810) 240109** 🕒 **Mon, Wed, Sat 8:30–2:30, Tue, Thu, Fri 8:30–2:30, 5:30–9**

Planet International
This is the largest bookshop in Irákleio Town and a good source for all sorts of English language books, including novels and guide books on Crete.
✉ **On the corner of Odós Hortatson and Odós Kidonias, behind Platía Venizélou** ☎ **(2810) 281558** 🕒 **Mon, Wed, Sat 8–2, Tue, Thu, Fri 8–2, 5:30–9**

Spirit of Greece
Appropriately located opposite the Archaeology Museum, this shop specialises in museum copies of ancient Greek pottery, particularly from the Minoan world. You can find Knosós-type *pithos* (storage jars), unusual stirrup jars and colourful Kamares-style cups, all at affordable prices. The artist, Vassilis Politakis, is in the shop every day at 4PM to talk about the Minoan art and his work in this ancient tradition.
✉ **Odós Papalexandrou 4** ☎ **(2810) 286287** 🕒 **Daily 10–6**

What to Buy
The best buys are traditional crafts – brightly coloured handwoven textiles, jewellery, ceramics, sculpture and leatherware. Although some of the 'crafts' sold in tourist areas are mass-produced and cheaply made, you still occasionally come across women working at looms, potters at the wheel or leather craftsmen making traditional knee-length boots.

Leather
Shops all over Crete sell leather goods, most of them made in Greece. Daidálos Street in Irákleio has very stylish shoes and leather jackets, but for cheaper leatherwork (bags, boots, belts, wallets) try the market in Irákleio and Odós Skrídlof in Chaniá which is entirely devoted to leather stalls. Villagers come here to buy handmade knee-length boots – fine quality but no bargain.

Pottery
The villages of Margaríites (east of Réthymno) and Thrapsanó (15km southeast of Kastélli, Irákleio) are long-established pottery-making centres, where you can visit the workshops and watch potters using ancient techniques. Some of them still make *pithoí*, the giant storage pots made on Crete since Minoan times. Not the ideal purchase to take back on the plane, but there are plenty of smaller souvenirs, and prices are lower than those of the shops.

Lasíthiou Province

Ágios Nikólaos
Byzántio
Most of the icons here are hand-painted and the artist who works here will explain the techniques, such as the cracking of the gold leaf to get the antique look. All of them are copies from old churches and monasteries throughout Greece. The icons come signed and with a certificate.

✉ **Odós 28 Októbriou 14**
☎ **(28410) 26530** 🕐 **Mon–Sat 10–2:30, 5–10; shorter hours in winter**

Ceramica 1
Nic Gabriel keeps the spirit of traditional Greek forms alive with his hand-made copies of ceramics from museums all over Greece. Each piece comes with a certificate of provenance and information about the history of the original. Shipping can be arranged.

✉ **Odós Paleólogou**
☎ **(28410) 24075** 🕐 **Daily 9:30AM–11PM. Closed winter**

Maria Patsaki
In a resort where so many shops sell souvenirs, this one stands out for its beautiful hand-woven textiles. Maria Patsaki has been here for 20 years, selling hand-woven bedcovers, rugs, carpets and beautiful fabrics which can be bought by the metre or made up to order (bedsets take two or three days and purchases can be sent abroad).

✉ **Odós K. Sfakianákis, 2**
☎ **(28410) 22001** 🕐 **Daily Apr–Oct 10–10 or later; winter 10–3 and 5–10**

Zoe
A good place to come for fun designer T-shirts for all ages decorated with motifs from Greek mythology. The shop, which is one of a chain, is English-run.

✉ **Odós Paleólogou 1**
☎ **(28410) 23962** 🕐 **8 or 9–10 depending on the tourist flow. Closed winter**

Eloúnta
Petrakis Icon Workshop
Artists Yiorgia and Ioannis Petrakis create beautifully painted icons using traditional materials and methods on Eloúnta's main street. Prices are very reasonable. They also sell a tasteful range of sculptures, jewellery and ceramics.

✉ **Odós A. Papandreou 22, Eloúnta** ☎ **(28410) 41669**
🕐 **Apr–Oct daily 10AM–11PM; phone for winter hours**

Réthymno Town
Brothers Kimionis
A family business operating since 1908, the Brothers Kimionis was the first shop to sell *rakí* in Crete. Today you'll find this a gourmet's delight packed with all kinds of spices, olive oils, honey, herbs and Cretan dictamus tea. Browsers may be lucky enough to be given a glass of *rakí* or a taste of local honey, but there is no obligation to buy.

✉ **Odós Paleologou 29–31, Réthymno** ☎ **(28310) 55667**

Kalymnos
Sponges of all shapes and sizes fill this delightful corner shop in the heart of the shopping district. Most of the stock comes from the Greek seas and lasts longer than cheaper varieties from

other countries.

✉ **Odós Arabatzoglou 26, Réthymno** ☎ **(28310) 50802**
🕓 **Daily 10AM–1AM**

La Bella Strada

This leather specialist near the Rimondi fountain sells high-quality bags of all descriptions.

✉ **Odós Paleologou 47, Réthymno** ☎ **(28310) 27592**
🕓 **Daily 10AM–late**

Chaniá Province

Chaniá Town

Carmela

This is more like a gallery than a shop. Carmela and her husband create beautiful ceramics and paintings, and there are original works of art from all over Greece made using traditional techniques.

✉ **Angeloú 7** ☎ **(28210) 90487** 🕓 **11–3, 6–10. Closed winter**

Artika

Stylish jeweller close to the Naval Museum. Beautiful necklaces (most made on the premises), earrings and brooches made of lapis lazuli and amber.

✉ **Odós Theotokopoúlou 63** ☎ **(28210) 91021** 🕓 **Daily 10–10. Closed winter**

Dimitris Savvakis

This is one of the many stalls you'll find in Chaniá covered market, selling a wide variety of herbs and spices. The speciality is the *koulouri*, the ornamental 'wedding bread' which is a symbol of friendship and love.

✉ **Chaniá Market (Dimotiki Agora 30)** ☎ **(28210) 41158**
🕓 **Mon, Wed, Thu Sat 8–2, Tue, Fri 8–1:30, 5–8**

Leather Alley

The street is almost entirely devoted to leather stalls. Choose from bags, belts, wallets, shoes, slippers and leather souvenirs. Much of it is made on the premises and the prices are reasonable.

✉ **Odós Skridlóf** 🕓 **Daily**

Local Artistic Handicrafts' Association

Craft items by 40 local artists displayed in a 200 year old building on Chaniá's harbour. The exhibits are not for sale, but staff will put you in touch with the workshops where they are made. Range includes ceramics, jewellery, embroidery, glass, knives, semi-precious stones and bronze characters from Greek mythology.

✉ **Odós Afendulief 14, Old Harbour, Chaniá** ☎ **(28210) 41885** 🕓 **Daily 9AM–10PM in season**

Roka Carpets

Wonderful selection of kilims, rugs and carpets – all hand-made by loom. If the shop is closed in winter knock on the door – except Sundays, which is the day for dying the wool.

✉ **Odós Zambelioú 61, Chaniá** ☎ **(28210) 74736** 🕓 **Daily 10–10; shorter hours in winter**

Top Hanas

Richly coloured, hand-woven Cretan bedspreads, kilims and tapestries, some of them over 100 years old, hung within an old Venetian building. Many of these were made for dowries.

✉ **Odós Angeloú 3 (near the Naval Museum)** ☎ **(28210) 98571** 🕓 **Daily 9:30–3, 5–9. Closed winter**

Herbs and Spices

Neatly packaged baskets of Cretan herbs and spices, sold in markets and food shops, make ideal gifts. Or take back some of the delicious aromatic Cretan honey, often sold in jars with nuts. Brothers Kimionis in Odós Paleologou, Réthymno, is an excellent place to shop for these. A family business since 1908, it is a gourmet's delight.

Icons

For a souvenir with a difference buy a Greek icon. These can be found all over the island and are normally reproductions of originals from churches and monasteries throughout Greece. The originals are hard to come by – and it's illegal to take them home.

Water Parks & Living History

Beach Safety
Some beaches can have dangerous currents. Follow the flag warning signals and swim in the designated areas. Protect children from the hot Mediterranean sun with a high protection sunscreen – particularly between the hours of 11AM and 3PM when the sun is at its hottest. Make sure children are also well protected when they are in the water.

The Cretans love children and welcome them with all the warmth and enthusiasm you would expect of a Mediterranean people. Apart from the water parks there are not many attractions that are specifically designed for children, but the island offers dozens of sandy beaches, sunshine for most of the year and sparkling blue waters for swimming and boat trips.

Away from the tourist resorts there are the added attractions of locals on donkeys, or mountain goats lingering in the middle of the road. For older children a wide variety of watersports facilities are available in all the main beach resorts (➤ 115) and a number of discos which are popular with teenagers.

Irákleio Province

Aqua Splash Water Park
Close to Limín Chersonísou, Aqua Splash offers rides down huge tubes and chutes or more leisurely journeys in rubber rings down the 'Lazy River'. There is also a tropical pool, children's pool and jacuzzi, and food outlets include Splash Food and Tropical Bars.

✉ Limín Chersonísou (on the road to Kastélli) ☎ (28970) 24950/1/2/3 🕐 May–Oct daily 10–7

Lychnostatis (Cretan Open-Air Museum)
If your children are unmoved by Minoan remains and archaeological museums try the Lychnostasis 'living museum' of Cretan traditional life. There are guided tours of an old stone

Cretan house, complete with workshops for weaving, pottery and wool dying, a restored windmill, a shepherd's shelter and a threshing floor.

The lovely gardens have pomegranates, prickly pears, loquats and vines, and there are 20 different Cretan aromatic herbs to see and smell (and you can taste them in beverages). Occasional special events include grape-treading for wine making, rakí distillation and on Saturdays evenings, Greek dancing and audio-visual shows.

✉ 1km from Limín Chersonísou ☎ (28970) 23660 🕐 Apr–Oct Tue–Sun 9:30–2 🚌 Service to Irákleio and Mália, bus stop 500m away

Star Water Park
In Limín Chersonísou, this huge beach and pool complex offers waterslides and numerous watersports facilities (water skiing, windsurfing, jet skis, banana rides, parasailing, scuba-diving, boat hire and bungee jumping) as well as aerobics, mini golf, volleyball and a children's play area. For those who prefer less active pursuits there are sunbeds, hydromassage, cocktail bars and a choice of places to eat. Admission is free and there are separate charges for the individual attractions.

✉ Beach Road, Limín Chersonísou ☎ (28970) 24472/3 🕐 Apr–Oct daily 10–7 🚌 Regular service to Irákleio and Mália

Water City
Equidistant from Irákleio and Limín Chersonísou (about 10 minutes by car) this is

Crete's most popular water-based leisure park. The large complex has huge water slides, chutes, crazy river rides, a wave pool, water polo and many other water-based activities. There is also a choice of bars and restaurants, shops, barbecue facilities and somewhere to change money.

✉ **Anópoli, Irákleio** ☎ **(2810) 781316** 🕑 **Apr–Sep daily 10–7** 🚍 **Service from Irákleio and Mália**

Lasíthiou Province

Municipal Beach Club, Ágios Nikólaos

Beyond the bus station on the south side of the town, the main town beach of Ágios Nikólaos has a club with mini golf, children's pool, playground, gardens and snack bar. Instructions are given in watersports. The beach is sandy and usually crowded.

✉ **Municipal Beach, Ágios Nikólaos** ☎ **None** 🕑 **Daily 10–6. Closed winter**

Spinalógka

Children enjoy the boat trip to the tiny island of Spinalógka (►51, 84) at the entrance to Eloúnta Bay. Some of the boat trips include swimming, and children can explore the island's fortress. The boats from Ágios Nikólaos pass the island of Agíi Pántes, a sanctuary of the Cretan wild goat.

Réthymno Province

Réthymno

There are a number of boat trips from Réthymno's harbour that are sure to capture children's imagination. Dolphin Cruises operate daily in summer for two- or three-hour trips, offering a chance to see dolphins along the north coast. The longer trips includes a stop at the villge of Panormo for a swim and lunch at one of the local tavernas. There are also daily sailings on two pirate ships. The *Barbarossa* cruises to Marathi with its secluded unspoiled beaches, while the *Captain Hook* sails to the resort of Bali, where you also stop for a swim. The crew dress as pirates and point out pirate caves, turtles and other sights. On board there are organised games, table games, fishing and snorkelling equipment, and even a spare pirate's costume.

✉ **Venetian Harbour, Réthymno** ☎ **(28310) 57666**

Chaniá Province

Georgioúpoli Boat Trips

The Almirós river flows into the sea at Georgioúpoli and you can take paddle boats or canoes along the river to see the turtles (hopefully) and a wide variety of birds, including kingfishers.

✉ **Georgioúpoli Beach – the boats are next to the chapel on the causeway of the beach**

Limnoupolis Water Park

This is the latest water park, in the west of the island, 8km south of Chaniá. Facilities include a wide range of aquatic activities, restaurant, bar and shopping arcade.

✉ **Varipetro, Chaniá** ☎ **(28210) 33224** 🕑 **May–Oct daily, all day** 🚍 **Regular bus service from Chaniá in season**

Eating Out

Few tavernas have special children's menus but there are plenty of places serving pasta and pizza. If you are eating Greek, firm favourites are *souvláki* (kebabs).

Bars, Discos, Clubs & Music

Bright Lights
Limín Chersonísou and Mália are the party capitals of Crete, with numerous neon-signed late-night bars and discos. Chaniá's nightlife is concentrated around the harbour, with jazz bars, cocktail bars and live Greek or international music in cafés and tavernas; Réthymno has its fare share of discos and music bars; and Ágios Nikólaos' harbour is the scene of lively, late-night bars and discos.

Irákleio Province

Ariadne
On the road to Knosós, offering dancing, live Greek music and restaurant.
✉ Knosós Avenue, Irákleio ☎ (2810) 231994 🕔 Summer only, 10PM–late

Arolithos
Open-air Cretan evenings with live music and dancing in full traditional costume. This takes place in a cleverly constructed 'traditional' Cretan village in the hills near Tílisos, where you can watch the local artisans in their workshops and buy their handmade goods.
✉ PO Box 2032 N Stadium 71002, Irákleio (11km southwest of Irákleio on the Old National Road) ☎ (2810) 821050; fax: (2810) 821051 🕔 Seasonal only, Mon–Fri, entertainment from 10PM until late into the night

Camelot
One of many discos in the late-night resort of Limín Chersonísou. You won't find many Cretans here but young tourists love it. Good music and dancing.
✉ Odós Minos, Limín Chersonísou, Irákleio ☎ (28970) 22734 🕔 Weekdays 11:30–4:30, weekends 11:30–6:30

Plateía Koraí
Plateía Koraí is the liveliest place in the town for an evening drink and is popular with young people. There are several casual bars with tables on the square, serving cocktails and other drinks. International and modern Greek music.
✉ Platía Koraí, Irákleio 🕔 Open all day, but liveliest after 9PM

Karouzanos Evening
Excursions are organised to the traditional mountain village of Karouzanos, near Kastélli. The evenings start with a glass of *rakí*, followed by a walk around the village, a drink in a *kafeníon* (traditional café) and a typical Cretan dinner in a local taverna, with free-flowing wine. The meal is accompanied by Cretan and Greek dancing.
Information from: ✉ Káto Karouzana Pediados, Irákleio ☎ (28910) 32404-5; fax: (28910) 32329 or ✉ Mareland Travel, Sanoudaki 16, Limín Chersonísou, Irákleio ☎ (28970) 24424; fax: (28970) 24150

Kazantzakis Theatre
This is an open-air venue for concerts, theatre and dance during Irákleio's summer festival. Some free performances.
✉ Jesus Bastion, near the Oasis Gardens ☎ (2810) 242977; fax: (2810) 227180 🕔 Jul–Sep; all performances start at 9:30

Lion's Bar
Called the Last Bar Before Africa (it would be if it weren't for the island of Gávdos), Lion's Bar has wonderful views of the sunset (and the sunrise). Twenty-one cocktails, music of all types and impromptu dancing. Meals available until late.
✉ Mátala Beach, Mátala, Irákleio ☎ (28920) 45759 🕔 All day and all night until 5 or later. Closed winter

Lasíthiou Province

Lipstick
Conspicuous disco on the harbour, popular with very

young tourists and locals.

✉ Akti Iosif Koundoúrou, Ágios Nikólaos, Lasíthiou
☎ (28410) 22377 🕓 10PM–late

Yanni's Rock Music Bar

Great music at this small, down-to-earth club at the end of the harbour, from classic 1970s and 80s rock to hard rock and blues.

✉ Akti Iosif Koundoúrou, Ágios Nikólaos, Lasíthiou
🕓 Daily from 10PM

Réthymno Province

Fortézza, Réthymno

Every summer, concerts, theatrical performances, ballet, recitals, traditional dance and song are performed at the Venetian fortress in Réthymno.

✉ Odós Katecháki, Réthymno
☎ (28310) 29148 🕓 mid-Jul to mid-Sep

Mouragio

This fish taverna, occupying a prime spot on Réthymno's harbour, has live Greek music every night with bouzoúkis, guitars and singing.

✉ Réthymno Harbour
🕓 8AM–3AM (music from 8PM–3AM)

Punch Bowl Irish Bar

Popular pub in a pretty street of the old town, serving Guinness, Amstel, Irish coffee and a long list of cocktails. Happy Hour (drinks at half price) from 8PM–10PM.

✉ Arabatzóglou 42, Réthymno
☎ (28320) 55572 🕓 6PM–late

Rock Cafe Club

It's good to see that locals and foreigners mix happily at this popular dance club in the heart of town.

✉ Odós Petiháki 8, Réthymno
☎ (28310) 31047 🕓 Daily 9PM–late

Chaniá Province

Fírkas Theatre

The courtyard of the Old Venetian Fortress is the setting for performances of traditional Greek dances, performed in costume.

✉ Fírkas Tower, Chaniá
☎ Information from the tourist office: (28210) 92943 🕓 Mon and Thu 9PM, summer only

Konaki

A taverna in the old town with live Greek music.

✉ Odós Kondilaki 40, Chaniá
☎ (28210) 70859 🕓 Daily

Kriti

Simple café near the Arsenal where you can listen to local music, and, if the mood takes you, get up and dance.

✉ Odós Kalergon 22, Chaniá
☎ None 🕓 Music from 9PM daily

Palace

Listen to Greek rock music on the roof garden on Chaniá's Venetian harbour with lovely views across to the lighthouse.

✉ Akti Tombázi, Old Harbour, Chaniá ☎ (28210) 45688
🕓 Daily 9PM–2:30AM

Fortezza

This restaurant/bar with music lies out by the lighthouse and has its own ferry to shuttle people across the harbour. The food is overpriced but it's fun to take the boat across or walk along the sea wall for a drink.

✉ Venetian Harbour, Chaniá
☎ (28210) 46546 🕓 Apr–Oct

Cretan Music

Cretans love to get up and dance and usually ensure that tourists all join in. The best-known instruments of Cretan folk music are the *lyra*, shaped like a mandolin and played with a bow, accompanied by the *laouto*, which is like a very big mandolin and has a deep bass sound. Normally the fancier the venue, the less authentic the performance.

Participatory Sports

Meltémi
Beware of the strong dry northerly wind known as the *Meltémi*, likely to hit Crete any time between June and September. The wind lingers for several days causing a drop in temperature, choppy seas and seaweed-strewn beaches.

Cycling
Hiring a bike is a pleasant way of exploring the island, but the hills and mountains make for strenuous pedalling. Cycle excursion companies can take away the strain by transporting the bikes up the mountains, allowing you to enjoy the scenic ride down. The cycling distances of the different excursions range from about 25 to 50km. The routes are mainly on surfaced roads and the cost includes guide, mountain bike, crash helmets, picnic and drinks.

Trekking Plan Outdoor Activities (for mountain bike hire and bike excursions) ✉ **Agía Marina, Neas Kidonias, Chaniá** ☎ **(28210) 60785; fax: (28210) 60861**

Diving
The warmth and crystal clear waters of the Cretan seas make excellent conditions for diving. Among the marine flora and fauna you are likely to see are sea anemones, sponges, small crabs, starfish, rock fish, octopus and moray eels. The waters are also excellent for snorkelling, and equipment can be hired or bought locally.

Scuba Kreta Diving Club
This well-equipped club organises a full range of regular PADI (Professional Association of Diving Instructors) courses. The taster session for the total beginner is a one-day course consisting of theory-pool dive and a sea dive to a maximum of 5–6m. The 4–5 day PADI full certificate course includes theory, confined water training and four sea dives. Divers with PADI or other internationally recognised certificates can participate in night diving, deep diving, cave diving or photo dives. The standards of safety are high, whether you are doing your first dive off the seashore or plunging 40m to the depths of the Mediterranean. The attractions include sunken wrecks and varied marine life.

✉ **Odós El. Venizelou, 60, Limín Chersonísou** ☎ **(28970) 24915; fax: (28970) 24916**

Golf
Currently the only opportunity for golfers is the 9-hole course at the Porto Eloúnta Resort, where tuition is available. There are plans in the pipeline to build several new golf courses on the island.

✉ **Porto Eloúnta Resort, Eloúnta, Lasíthiou** ☎ **(28410) 41903; fax: (28410) 41889**

Horse Riding
Horse riding and riding lessons are available at clubs in or near the four main centres of Irákleio, Ágios Nikólaos, Réthymno and Chaniá.

Club Karterós
Opportunities for exploring the countryside on horseback. Also riding lessons and horse and wagon tours.

✉ **Amnisos-Karterós Beach, Irákleio** ☎ **(2810) 380244**

Nteres Horse-Riding Centre
In a remote location, this riding centre offers accompanied tours in the mountains. Facilities include a café and restaurant.

✉ **Nteres, Chaniá** ☎ **(28240) 31339 fax: (28240) 31900**

Walking And Climbing

With its scenic gorges, mountains and valleys Crete provides plenty of opportunities for walking and climbing. The most famous walk is the 16km Samariá Gorge (▶ 20, 83). Less crowded and half the length are the Impros Gorge (▶ 82) and the Agía Irini Gorgeá. Only serious climbers should tackle the Lefká Óri (White Mountains) or Crete's highest peak, Timíos Stavrós (2,456m).

The Happy Walker

Six different walks, organised in small groups and escorted by an experienced guide. The walks last about four hours and end with lunch in a village taverna. Transport is provided to the starting point.

✉ **Odós Tombasi, 56, Réthymno (in the old town, near the Metropolis church)**
☎ **(28310) 52920**

Káto Mirabello Trekking

A booklet supplied by the tourist office at Ágios Nikólaos gives maps and details of 17 walks (or bike routes), starting from the main coastal and inland centres of the region (such as Ágios Nikólaos, Eloúnta or Kritsá). The tracks are marked and the leaflet highlights points of natural and archaeological interest, as well as cafés and tavernas.

🛈 **Ágios Nikólaos** ☎ **(28410) 22357**

Greek Climbing Club (Eos)

The club operates refuges in the White Mountains (☎ (28210) 54560) and at Psiloreítis. It also has information on skiing in the Cretan mountains.

✉ **Odós Dikeiosínis 53, 71201 Irákleio** ☎ **(2810) 227609**
✉ **Odós Tzanakaki, 90, 73100 Chaniá** ☎ **(2810) 44647**
✉ **Odós Moatsou, 74100 Réthymno** ☎ **(28310) 22710**

Watersports and Swimming

The sandy beaches and warm, clear waters are excellent for swimming. The main season for watersports is from late May to late October. The larger resort beaches, such as Mália, Ágios Nikólaos and the strip west of Chaniá, offer a choice of watersports such as wind-surfing (with instruction and board-hire), pedaloes, banana boats and jet skis. De luxe hotels also have a wide range: the Sofitel Capsis Palace and Capsis Beach Resort Hotel at Agía Pelagia has a wind-surfing school, waterskiing, jet skis, pedaloes, canoes and banana boat rides. In the east the Club Nautique at the Eloúnta Beach Hotel has parasailing, waterskiing, diving, windsurfing, sailing, pedaloes and canoes. Such hotels can also organise excursions in glass bottom boats, speedboats with a driver, yachts with a skipper and bar, fishing trips and other ideas.

Sofitel Capsis Palace and Capsis Beach Resort Hotel

✉ **Agía Pelagía**
☎ **(2810) 811212; fax: (2810) 811076**

Eloúnta Beach Hotel

✉ **72100 Ágios Nikólaos**
☎ **(28410) 41412; fax: (28410) 41373**

Diving

To protect antiquities, diving independently of a club in Greek waters is forbidden. Half a dozen specific areas in Crete are exempt from the ban including Eloúnta (information from Eloúnta Beach Hotel, ☎ (28410) 41412) and Réthymno (information from Paradise Dive Centre, El Venizélou, 73 ☎ 28310 26317). Divers are strictly forbidden to remove any antiquities from the sea bed, or even to take photographs of them.

What's On When

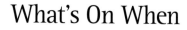

Festivals

The Greeks have a passion for festivals and fairs, and the Cretans are no exception. Villages celebrate their saint's name day with parades, fireworks, singing and dancing. While some of the island's festivals are strictly religious, others are aimed primarily at tourists. Either way the celebrations are very colourful events.

January

New Year's Day (1 Jan): processions, traditional seasonal songs and cutting of the New Year's Cake to find the lucky coin.
Epiphany (6 Jan): blessings of the water; crosses thrown into the sea.

March

Katharí Deftéri 'Clean Monday' (last Monday before Lent): celebrations marking the end of Carnival and beginning of Lent.
Independence Day (25 Mar): military parades.
Holy Week. Greek Orthodox Easter falls up to four weeks either side of the Western festival. This is the most important religious festival in Greece, celebrated with church services, processions, dancing, singing, feasting and fireworks.

May

Labour Day (1 May): parades and flower festivals.
Commemorations of the Battle of Crete (20–27 May), celebrated in Chaniá.

July

There are festivals and folk performances all over Crete during the busy summer season. Local tourist offices can provide you with information. Irákleio has a summer festival of music, opera, drama, ballet, dancing and jazz.
Cretan Wine Festival (mid-Jul): a week of wine tasting and dancing in Réthymno.

August

Fair in Anógia (6 Aug).
Sultana Festival (mid-Aug), in Siteía.
Feast of the Assumption (15 Aug).
Pilgrimage for those named Ioánnis (John) to the Church of Ágios Ioánnis on the Rodoúpou peninsula, Chaniá (29 Aug).
Summer in Chaniá: music, dance, shows.
Renaissance Festival: music, drama and films at the Venetian fortress in Réthymno.

October

Chestnut Festival (mid-Oct), in Élos and other villages of southwest Crete.
Óchi Day ('No' Day, 28 Oct): commemorating the day the Greeks turned down Mussolini's ultimatum in World War II.

November

Commemoration in Réthymno and Arkádi of the destruction of the Arkádi monastery in 1866 by the Turks (7–9 Nov).
Feast of the Presentation of the Virgin in the Temple (21 Nov), in Réthymno

December

Christmas Day (25 Dec): a feast day, but less significant to the Cretans than Easter.
St Stephen's Day (26 Dec).

Practical
Matters

Above: *olive
groves on the
Lasíthiou plain*
Right: *a donkey
takes a well earned
break*

117

TIME DIFFERENCES

GMT 12 noon	Crete 2PM	Germany 1PM	USA (NY) 7AM	Netherlands 1PM	Spain 1PM

BEFORE YOU GO

WHAT YOU NEED

● Required
○ Suggested
▲ Not required

Some countries require a passport to remain valid for a minimum period (usually at least six months) beyond the date of entry – contact their consulate or embassy or your travel agent for details.

	UK	Germany	USA	Netherlands	Spain
Passport/National Identity Card	●	●	●	●	●
Visa (regulations can change – check beofre booking your trip)	▲	▲	▲	▲	▲
Onward or Return Ticket	▲	▲	▲	▲	▲
Health Inoculations	○	○	○	○	○
Health Documentation – Reciprocal Agreements (► 123, Health)	●	●	▲	●	●
Travel Insurance	●	●	●	●	●
Driving Licence (National or International)	●	●	●	●	●
Car Insurance Certificate (if own car)	●	●	●	●	●
Car Registration Document (if own car)	●	●	●	●	●

WHEN TO GO

Crete

█████ High season

▭ Low season

12°C	12°C	14°C	17°C	20°C	24°C	26°C	26°C	24°C	21°C	17°C	14°C
JAN	FEB	MAR	APR	MAY	JUN	JUL	AUG	SEP	OCT	NOV	DEC

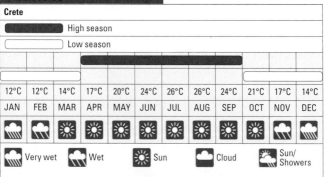

🌧 Very wet   🌧 Wet   ☀ Sun   ☁ Cloud   ⛅ Sun/Showers

TOURIST OFFICES

In the UK
Greek National Tourist
Organisation
(GNTO/EOT)
4 Conduit Street
London W1R 0DJ
☎ 020 7734 5997
Fax: 020 7287 1369

In the USA
GNTO/EOT
Olympic Tower
645 Fifth Avenue
New York
NY 10022
☎ 212/ 421 5777
Fax: 212/826 6940

In Canada
GNTO/EOT
1170 Place du Frère André
Suite 300
Montréal, Quebec
H3B 3C6
☎ 514/871 1535
Fax: 514/871 1498

ARRIVING

The majority of direct flights to Crete are charters from major European cities, available only from April to October. Tour operators fly mainly to Irákleio, though some also use Chaniá airport for resorts in western Crete. There are scheduled flights to Athens from Europe and the USA, with connections to Crete.

Irákleio Airport	Journey Times
Kilometres to city centre	🛫 N/A
	🚌 15 minutes
5 kilometres	🚗 10 minutes

Chaniá Airport	Journey times
Kilometres to city centre	🛫 N/A
	🚌 20 minutes
12 kilometres	🚗 15 minutes

MONEY

The euro (€) is the official currency of Greece. Euro banknotes and coins were introduced in January 2002. Banknotes are issued in denominations of 5, 10, 20, 50, 100, 200 and 500 euros; coins in denominations of 1, 2, 5, 10, 20 and 50 cents, and 1 and 2 euros.

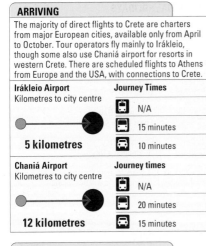

TIME

 Crete is two hours ahead of Greenwich Mean Time (GMT + 2). The clocks go forward one hour on the last Sunday in March and back one hour on the last Sunday in October.

CUSTOMS

YES
From another EU country for personal use (guidelines):
800 cigarettes, 200 cigars, 1 kilogram of tobacco
10 litres of spirits (over 22%)
20 litres of aperitifs
90 litres of wine, of which 60 litres can be sparkling wine
110 litres of beer

From a non-EU country for your personal use, the allowances are:
200 cigarettes OR
50 cigars OR
250 grams of tobacco
1 litre of spirits (over 22%)
2 litres of intermediary products (eg sherry) and sparkling wine
2 litres of still wine
50 grams of perfume
0.25 litres of eau de toilette

The value limit for goods is 175 euros

Travellers under 17 years of age are not entitled to the tobacco and alcohol allowances.

NO
Drugs, firearms, ammunition, offensive weapons, obscene material, unlicensed animals.

EMBASSIES AND CONSULATES

UK (2810) 224012 (Irákleio)	**Germany** (2810) 226288 (Irákleio) (28210) 57944 (Chaniá)	**Netherlands** (2810) 346202 (Irákleio)	**USA** (Athens Embassy) (210) 721 2951	**France** (28210) 91191 (Chaniá)

WHEN YOU ARE THERE

TOURIST OFFICES

- Odós Xanthoudídou, 1
  Platía Elefthérias (opposite
  Archaeological Museum)
  Irákleio
  ☎ (2810) 228225 or 228203;
  fax: (2810) 226020

- Irákleio Airport
  Irákleio
  ☎ (2810) 244462

- Odós Aktí I. Koundoúrou,
  20 (between the lake and
  the harbour)
  Ágios Nikólaos, Lasíthiou
  ☎ (28410) 22357; fax:
  (28410) 82534

- Palaikastro
  Siteía 72300, Lasíthiou
  ☎ (28430) 61225; fax:
  (28430) 61230

- Prikiméa Eleftthérios
  Venizélos (on the seafront
  east of the harbour)
  Réthymno
  ☎ (28310) 29148; fax:
  (28310) 56350

- Megaro Pantheon Building
  Odós Kriári 40 (just east of
  Platía 1866)
  Chaniá
  ☎ (28210) 92943; fax:
  (28210) 92624

- Venizélos Street
  Palaióchora
  Chaniá
  ☎ (28230) 41507

- Waterfront, near Plateía
  Polytechniou
  Siteía,
  Lasíthiou
  ☎ (28430) 28300

NATIONAL HOLIDAYS

J	F	M	A	M	J	J	A	S	O	N	D
2	(1)	1(2)	(1)	1(1)	(1)		1		1		2

1 Jan	New Year's Day
6 Jan	Epiphany
Feb/Mar	'Clean Monday'
25 Mar	Independence Day
Mar/Apr	Good Friday and Easter Monday
1 May	Labour Day
May/Jun	Ascension Day
15 Aug	Feast of the Assumption
28 Oct	Óchi Day
25 Dec	Christmas Day
26 Dec	St Stephen's Day

Restaurants and some tourists shops may stay open
on these days, but museums will be closed.

OPENING HOURS

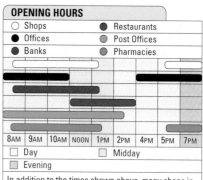

In addition to the times shown above, many shops in
tourist areas stay open daily from 8AM to late evening
throughout the season but close or have shorter
hours in winter.
Many restaurants stay open all day during the holiday
season. Post offices in Irákleio and Chaniá are open
7:30–7:30. Banks close on Saturdays, Sundays and
public holidays.
The opening hours of museums and archaeological
sites vary enormously but the majority are closed
on Mondays.

DRIVE ON THE RIGHT

TOILETS FREE

★★ ★★

PUBLIC TRANSPORT

 Buses Crete has an extensive network of buses, providing a cheap and reasonably reliable service throughout the island. There is an excellent service along the main highway linking Ágios Nikólaos, Irákleio, Réthymno and Chaniá, with buses at least every hour. From these towns there are services to smaller towns and most villages. Irákleio has three bus stations, operating services to different regions. Only buses within Irákleio are numbered – others show the destination (not always the right one) on the front of the bus. Local bus timetables are available from bus stations, local tourist offices and sometimes at bus stops. You need to flag down the bus as it approaches.

 Ferries and Boat Trips Ferries connect Irákleio, Chaniá and Ágios Nikólaos with the mainland at Piraeus and with other islands such as Rhodes and Santarini. Boat excursions operate from May to October. Popular trips include cruises to the offshore islands of Spinalógka, Yaidouronísi (Chrysí) and Diá.
From Chaniá there are day excursions to the Diktýnna Temple, and from several resorts there are boat trips to unspoilt and otherwise inaccessible beaches. Ferries link the south coast resorts of Palaióchora, Soúyia, Agía Rouméli, Loutró and Chora Sfakíon. From Soúyia, Palaióchora and Chora Sfakíon ferries operate to the island of Gávdos south of Crete.

 Urban Transport Irákleio is the only major conurbation on Crete but because of the one-way system and the central location of the sites and shops, most tourists tend to walk. The city has three bus stations, operating services to different regions of Crete. Buses for Knosós leave from a stop adjacent to the east-bound bus station.

CAR RENTAL

Crete has numerous car rental firms, including all the internationally known names. Hire rates are generally reasonable by European standards, particularly off-season. Check they include tax, collision damage waivers and unlimited mileage.

TAXIS

 Taxis on Crete are plentiful and can be hailed in the street or picked up at taxi ranks. Check the meter is switched on or, if there is no meter, agree a price in advance. There are some fixed price journeys within towns and from the airports.

DRIVING

Speed limit on national highway: **100kph** for cars

Speed limit on country roads: **80kph**

Speed limit in built-up areas: **50kph**

Seat belts must be worn in both front and rear seats. Children under 10 must sit in the rear.

Drink-driving is heavily penalised. Tolerance is a blood alcohol level of 0.05 per cent of alcohol.

Petrol is readily available in the towns, but it's wise to fill up if you are touring. Super (95 octane), unleaded, super unleaded and diesel are available. Service stations are open Mon–Fri, 7AM–7PM, Sat 7AM–3PM. Some stay open until midnight and open Sun 7AM–7PM.

Members of motoring organisations are entitled to free breakdown service from the Greek motoring organisation, ELPA, ☎ 104 in emergencies. Non-members should dial 174 for assistance. Car hire companies should also be notified as most will have their own procedures.

PERSONAL SAFETY

The crime rate in Crete is very low. Visitors can stroll through the streets without any threat, though unescorted women should not be surprised if they attract the Mediterranean roving eye. Whilst petty crime is minimal, it's wise to take simple precautions:

- Safeguard against attracting the attention of pickpockets.
- Leave valuables and important documents in the hotel or apartment safe.
- Lock car doors and never leave valuables visible inside.

Police assistance:

☎ **100**
from any call box

TELEPHONES

Public telephones take a phone card, available locally in units of 100, 200, 500 and 1000. Some kiosks, shops and cafés have telephones with meters that can be used for international calls. OTE (Greek Telecom) have telephone exchanges in the larger resorts where you can make calls from booths and pay in cash afterwards.

International Dialling Codes

From Crete dial	
UK:	00 44
Germany:	00 49
USA & Canada:	00 1
Netherlands:	00 31
Spain:	00 34

POST

Post offices in the towns and larger villages are identified by yellow signs. In summer mobile offices operate in tourist areas. Post offices usually open 7:30–2:30 Mon–Fri, but in Irákleio and Chaniá they're open until 7:30. Some mobile post offices also open at weekends. Stamps can be bought at shops or kiosks selling postcards.

ELECTRICITY

The power supply is 220 volts AC, 50hz.
Type of socket: 2 round-

hole type, taking continental 2-pin plug.
Visitors from the UK should bring an adaptor. Visitors from the USA will need a transformer for appliances using different voltages.

TIPS/GRATUITIES

Yes ✓ No ✗		
Hotels (if service not inc.)	✓	10%
Restaurants (if service not inc.)	✓	10%
Cafés/Bars (if service not inc.)	✓	10%
Taxis	✓	Change
Porters	✓	50 cents a bag
Tour Guides	✓	Discretionary
Cinema Usherettes	✗	
Hairdressers	✓	10%
Toilets	✓	Discretionary

What to photograph: deep blue seas, cliffs, mountains and gorges; harbours, rustic villages, locals in traditional costume, mountain goats.
Where it is forbidden: in some museums, near military bases and in churches and monasteries where icons require flash.
Where to buy film: the most popular brands of colour print or transparency film are available from kiosks and shops.

HEALTH

Insurance
Visitors from the European Union (EU) are entitled to reciprocal state medical care in Greece and should take with them a form E111 available from post offices. However, this covers treatment in only the most basic of hospitals and private medical insurance is advisable.

Dental Services
Dental treatment must be paid for by all visitors. Hotels can normally provide names of local English-speaking dentists; alternatively ask your Consulate. Private medical insurance is strongly advised to cover the cost of dental treatment.

Sun Advice
Crete enjoys sunshine for most of the year, and from April/May until September it is almost constant. During July and August, when the sun is at its hottest, a hat, strong-protection sunscreen and plenty of non-alcoholic fluids are recommended.

Drugs
Pharmacies have a large green or red cross outside the shop and sell most internationally known drugs and medicines over the counter or by prescription. Most pharmacies have someone who can speak English. Opening hours are the same as those of shops, with a rota system at weekends.

Safe Water
Tap water is quite safe but because of the high level of minerals it does not suit all tourists. Bottled water is available everywhere at a reasonable cost.

CONCESSIONS

Students/Youths Holders of an International Student Identity Card (ISIC) are entitled to substantial reductions on entrance fees to museums and archaeological sites. Very cheap accommodation is available in youth hostels at Irákleio, Ágios Nikólaos, Réthymno, Chaniá, Siteía and other towns, but early reservations for the summer months are essential.

Senior Citizens Most museums and archaeological sites have reduced rates for elderly visitors. There are few other concessions but senior citizens can take advantage of the off-season rates in spring and October – the ideal times to visit the island.

GREEK ALPHABET

The Greek alphabet cannot be transliterated into other languages in a straightforward way. This can lead to variations in romanised spellings of Greek words and place-names. It also leads inevitably to inconsistencies, especially when comparing different guide books, leaflets and signs. However, the differences rarely make any name unrecognisable. The language looks complex, but it is worth memorising the alphabet to help with signs, destinations etc.

Alpha	Αα	short a, as in hat
Beta	Ββ	v sound
Gamma	Γγ	guttural g sound
Delta	Δδ	hard th, as in father
Epsilon	Εε	short e
Zita	Ζζ	z sound
Eta	Ηη	long e, as in feet
Theta	Θθ	soft th, as in think
Iota	Ιι	short i, as in hit
Kappa	Κκ	k sound
Lambda	Λλ	l sound
Mu	Μμ	m sound
Nu	Νν	n sound
Xi	Ξξ	x or ks sound
Omicron	Οο	short o, as in pot
Pi	Ππ	p sound
Rho	Ρρ	r sound
Sigma	Σσ	s sound
Tau	Ττ	t sound
Upsilon	Υυ	ee, or y as in funny
Phi	Φφ	f sound
Chi	Χχ	guttural ch, as in loch
Psi	Ψψ	ps, as in chops
Omega	Ωω	long o, as in bone

- Contact the airport, airline or travel representative 72 hours prior to leaving to ensure flights are unchanged.
- Arrive 90 minutes before your scheduled flight departure time, particularly in high season. Make sure you have all necessary documentation ready.
- Antiquities may not be taken out of Crete.

LANGUAGE

The official language of Crete is Greek. Many of the locals speak English, but a few words of Greek can be useful in rural areas where locals may know no English. It is also useful to know the Greek alphabet – particularly for reading street names and road signs (▶ 123). A few useful words and phrases are listed below, with phonetic transliterations and accents to show emphasis. More words and phrases can be found in the AA *Essential Greek Phrase Book*. Because the method of translating Greek place names has changed recently, some spellings may differ from older ones you find on the island.

	hotel	xenodhohío	toilet	twaléta
	room	dhomátyo	bath	bányo
	...single/double	monó/dhipló	shower	doos
	for three people	ya tría átoma	hot water	zestó neró
	can I see it?	boró na to dho?	balcony	balkóni
	breakfast	proinó	campsite	kamping
	guest house	pansyón	key	klidhí
	toilet paper	charti iyías	towel	petséta

	bank	trápeza	credit card	pistotikí kárta
	exchange office	ghrafío sinalágh-matos	traveller's cheque	taxidhyotikí epitayí
	post office	tahidhromío	passport	dhiavatíryn
	money	leftá	can I pay by...?	boró na plíroso me...?
	cash desk	tamío		
	how much?	póso káni?	cheap	ftinós
	exchange rate	isotimía	expensive	akrivós

	restaurant	estiatório	bread	psomi
	café	kafenío	water	nero
	menu	menóo	wine	krasi
	lunch	yévma	coffee	kafés
	dinner	dhípno	fruit	fróoto
	dessert	epidhórpyo	coffee	kafés
	waiter	garsóni	waitress	servitóra
	the bill	loghariazmós	tea (black)	tsái

	aeroplane	aeropláno	...single/return	apló/metepistrofís
	airport	aerodhrómio		
	bus	leoforío	car	aftokínito
	...station	stathmós	taxi	taxí
	...stop	stási	the road to...	o dhrómos ya
	boat	karávi	no smoking	mi kapnízondes
	...port/harbour	limáni	timetable	dhromolóyo
	ticket	isitírio	petrol	venzíni

	yes	né	goodbye	....adío or yásas, yásoo
	no	óhi		
	please	parakaló	sorry	signómi
	thank you	efharistó	how much?	póso káni?
	hello	yásas, yásoo	where is...?	poú eené..?
	good morning	kalí méra	help!	voíthia!
	good evening	kalí spéra	my name is...	meh léne
	good night	kalí níkhta	I don't speak Greek	then miló hellniká
	I don't understand	katalavéno	excuse me	me sinchoríte

INDEX

Acknowledgements
The Automobile Association wishes to thank the following photographers, libraries and
associations for their assistance in the preparation of this book.

IRÁKLEIO ARCHAEOLOGICAL MUSEUM 8b, 15b, 17b, 17c; HULTON GETTY 14c; NATURE
PHOTOGRAPHERS LTD 13b (R Tidman) S OUTRAM 39a; SPECTRUM COLOUR LIBRARY 42/3;
WORLD PICTURES 1; www.euro.ecb.int/ 119 (euro notes).

The remaining pictures are held in the Association's own library (**AA PHOTO LIBRARY**) and were
taken by KEN PATERSON with the exception of the following pages:
S. L. DAY 122b; **P. ENTICKNAP** 2, 9b, 9d, 10b, 12b, 12c, 13a, 18b, 19b, 21b, 22/3, 23, 24/5, 25b,
27b, 28/9, 31c, 34a, 34b, 38a, 38c, 46a, 47b, 48b, 61b, 62, 63, 65a, 65b, 66a, 68a, 71a, 71b, 72a,
74, 75, 76a, 76/7, 77, 78, 79a, 80a, 80b, 81, 83a, 84a, 85b, 85c, 86, 87, 88a, 89a, 90a, 92a, 93b;
T. HARRIS 72b, 73a, 84b; **S. OUTRAM** 122a, 122b

Updated by: Donna Dailey   Page layout: Design23
Revision Management: Apostrophe S Limited

Dear Essential Traveller

Your comments, opinions and recommendations are very important to us. So please help us to improve our travel guides by taking a few minutes to complete this simple questionnaire.

You do not need a stamp (unless posted outside the UK). If you do not want to cut this page from your guide, then photocopy it or write your answers on a plain sheet of paper.

Send to: **The Editor, AA World Travel Guides, FREEPOST SCE 4598, Basingstoke RG21 4GY.**

Your recommendations…

We always encourage readers' recommendations for restaurants, nightlife or shopping – if your recommendation is used in the next edition of the guide, we will send you a *FREE* AA *Essential* **Guide** of your choice. Please state below the establishment name, location and your reasons for recommending it.

_____

_____

_____

_____

Please send me **AA *Essential*** _____

(*see list of titles inside the front cover*)

About this guide…

Which title did you buy?

AA *Essential* _____

Where did you buy it? _____

When? <u>m m</u> / <u>y y</u>

Why did you choose an AA *Essential* Guide? _____

_____

_____

_____

_____

Did this guide meet your expectations?

Exceeded ☐ Met all ☐ Met most ☐ Fell below ☐

Please give your reasons _____

_____

_____

_____

continued on next page…

Were there any aspects of this guide that you particularly liked? _____

_____

_____

_____

Is there anything we could have done better? _____

_____

_____

_____

_____

About you...

Name (*Mr/Mrs/Ms*) _____

   Address _____

_____

_____ Postcode _____

   Daytime tel nos _____

Which age group are you in?
   Under 25 ☐ 25–34 ☐ 35–44 ☐ 45–54 ☐ 55–64 ☐ 65+ ☐

How many trips do you make a year?
   Less than one ☐ One ☐ Two ☐ Three or more ☐

Are you an AA member? Yes ☐ No ☐

About your trip...

When did you book? m m / y y   When did you travel? m m / y y
How long did you stay? _____
Was it for business or leisure? _____
Did you buy any other travel guides for your trip?
   If yes, which ones? _____

_____

Thank you for taking the time to complete this questionnaire. Please send
it to us as soon as possible, and remember, you do not need a stamp
(*unless posted outside the UK*).

Happy Holidays!